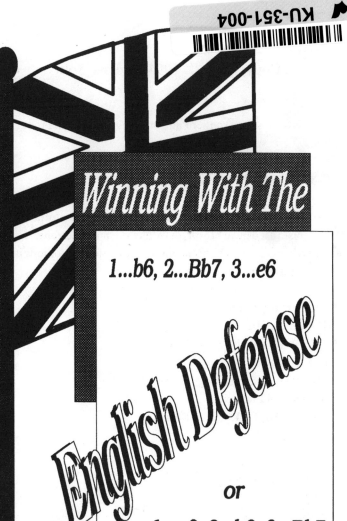

Winning With The

1...b6, 2...Bb7, 3...e6

English Defense

or

1...e6, 2...b6, 3...Bb7

GM Andrew Soltis

Chess Digest, Inc

Copyright © 1994 Andrew Soltis

ISBN: 0-87568-257-X

AUTHOR: Andrew Soltis
EDITOR: Ken Smith
COMPUTER TYPESET: Sid Pickard
COVER: Elaine Smith
FINAL PROOF: Sid Pickard and David Sewell
DIAGRAMS: Sid Pickard
FINAL PREPARATION: Ken Smith

PUBLISHER: Chess Digest, Inc. ® , 1601 Tantor, Dallas, Texas 75229

Send the publisher $2.00 for the *New Chess Guide* that catalogs every chess book for general sale in the United States. You are given publishers, page counts, notation, and critical reviews. Also included is a free Chess Improvement Course for beginners up through Master level players.

TABLE OF CONTENTS

INTRODUCTION
1...b6 then 2...e6 or
1...e6 then 2...b6

There is, it's often been said, nothing new under the sun. In chess openings this is constantly being verified as players discover antecedents for what they had considered new ideas. At least once a month, it seems, some grandmaster takes credit for a TN – unaware that it had been played before, sometimes thirty or forty years before.

In the case of the English Defense, we can see how an opening that was tested 100 and even 150 years ago is being rediscovered by modern masters unaware that it was even played before 1975.

The English Defense has had, in fact, a remarkably long history. It was briefly popular in the mid-19th century and not revived until the 1970's. In between it was a specialty opening, used chiefly by players trying to establish their originality – or players who didn't know any better when they held the Black pieces.

Black's basic strategy when he opens 1...b6 is to control e4 with ...Bb7. As the English Defense evolved, a number of positional ideas were added to it besides the fianchetto. Among them, as we'll see, is the pinning ...Bb4 if White dares bring his b1-Knight out to its best square, and the flanking pawn attack ...f7-f5. There are, particularly after 1.d4 b6, some remarkable Queen moves that Black can play with more than psychological effect. Whenever you examine really old openings it's worth recalling that they were tested by some fairly good opponents. If Paul Morphy couldn't come up with anything better than 4.Nh3, in the game below, that might indicate the true strength of Black's system.

Morphy-Owen, London 1858

1.e4	b6
2.d4	Bb7
3.Bd3	e6
4.Nh3	

Geza Maroczy, and other commentators on Morphy's games, didn't like this strange move, which has a very 1850-ish look. Among the useful, relatively noncommittal moves at White's disposal are 4.c3 and 4.Nd2.

4...   c5!

5.c3   cxd4

Normally we would consider this exchange premature. But the Reverend Owen, who did so much to put life into 1...b6, had a particular plan in mind: he wanted to exploit the b4 and d4 squares.

6.cxd4   Nc6

7.Be3   Nb4

This is Owen's idea, which recurs in many similar positions: thanks to White's third and fourth moves, the two center pawns are vulnerable – and so is the Bishop to ...Nxd3 + .

8.Nc3   Nxd3 +

9.Qxd3   Bb4

Black hastens to put pressure on e4 with his minor pieces (...Nf6).

10.0-0   Bxc3?

But this gives White back the control of d5 he needs and deprives Black of the dark-squared Bishop he needs. Better is simply 10...Nf6, threatening 11...Bxc3 and 12...Bxe4. Naturally, on 10...Nf6 11.e5 Black will land on d5.

11.bxc3   Nf6

12.e5!

But now the Knight can be driven off d5 by the newly created c-pawn.

12...	**Nd5**
13.c4	**Ba6**

And here 13...Nxe3 looks correct. The e3-Bishop isn't impressive now but it will be when it reaches the a3-f8 diagonal.

14.Bd2	**Rc8**
15.Rac1	**0-0**
16.Qb3	**Ne7**
17.Bb4	

White's advantage, due to his control of the dark squares, is clear. The only thing bad about his game – is that dumb Knight, still on h3.

17...	**Re8**
18.Rfd1	**Nf5**
19.g4!?	

With this White chooses his middlegame plan – a Kingside advance. He may have done better with 19.d5. Instead of closing the h1-a8 diagonal, White now opens it.

19...	**Nh4**
20.f4	**f6!**
21.Be1	**fxe5**
22.dxe5	

This looks clearly wrong. Whatever benefit is derived from the opening of the d-file is offset by the isolation of the c-pawn and the opening of the g1-c5 diagonal.

22...	**Qe7**
23.Ng5	**h6**

So that 24.Bxh4 hxg5 25.Bxg5 can be met by 25...Qc5 + .

24.Ne4	**Bb7**
25.Qd3	**Rf8**

White has been trying to exploit the "Knight-on-the-rim". Here 26.Nf6 + seems to do the trick, but then Black has 26...gxf6, meeting 27.Bxh4 with 27...Qc5 + 28.Bf2 Qc6. So White tries another way.

26.Bxh4!	**Qxh4**

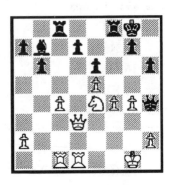

27.Nf6 +	**Rxf6!**

Of course, not 27...gxf6 28.Qg6 + and 29.Rxd7.

28.exf6	**Qxg4 +**
29.Qg3	**Qxg3 +**
30.hxg3	

For his sacrificed Exchange Black has a nice pawn and – perhaps more important – the ability to block files. White's Rooks don't constitute an advantage until they have open files.

30...	**Bc6!**
31.fxg7	**Kxg7**
32.Kf2	**Kf6**
33.g4?	

This helps the enemy out. With 33.Re1 and 34.Re5 White begins to penetrate, according to Maroczy.

33...	**h5!**
34.g5 +	**Kf5**

Now 35.Kg3 Rh8 gives Black the upper hand thanks to his King and mobile h-pawn.

35.Ke3	**h4**
36.Rd2	**h3**

After this and ...Bg2, White has no Exchange advantage anymore and must consider ways to force a draw.

37.Rh2	**Bg2**
38.Rc2	**d5!**

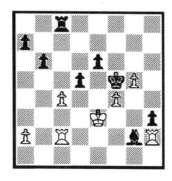

Winning a pawn and assuring victory. Now 39.Kd4 Kxf4 40.g6 e5+ must be lost for White.

39.g6!	**dxc4**
40.g7	**Rg8**
41.Rcxg2	

This had to happen at some point. The Bishop that started out on c8 had quite an influence on this game.

41...	**hxg2**
42.Rxg2	**Kf6**

Black probably didn't like 42...e5 because of 43.Rg5+.

43.Rc2	**Rxg7**
44.Rxc4	**Rg3+**
45.Ke4	**Ra3**

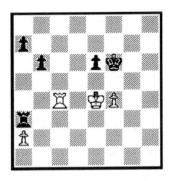

This ties down the Rook and prepares the King's entrance at f5.

46.Rc2   Ra4 +

White resigns

But as usual with irregular openings, the strategically confusing English Defense needed confusing English strategists to survive. Once the generation of Rev. John Owen and Samuel Standidge Boden had passed on, there were no worthy masters to carry on the 1...b6 tradition.

In addition, theory was paying more and more attention to 1.d4 by the turn of the century, and it was not at all clear that 1...b6 was as good an answer to that move as it was in Morphy's day to 1.e4.

By the 1920's Aron Nimzovich had developed an opening system – not just a variation of an opening – but an entire system based on meeting 1.d4 with a fight for control of e4. Nimzovich's system called for 1...Nf6 2.c4 e6. Then if White controlled e4 with 3.Nc3, Black must immediately stop the advance of the e-pawn with 3...Bb4, he reasoned. If White avoided the pin with 3.Nf3, Black could contest e4 by means of 3...b6 and 4...Bb7.

Nimzovich's system – today known as the Nimzo-Indian Defense and Queen's Indian Defense – proved enormously popular. Yet there was a slightly different defense, also based on the fight for e4 with ...Bb7, that emerged. In this defense, begun by 1...b6, Black could not prevent e2-e4. But, in return, Black obtained some new tactical options. By not developing his Knight on f6, Black could bring out his Queen early on, or advance his f-pawn to attack the enemy center.

A rare early illustration of Black's strategy is this:

Dobias-Graf, Prague 1937

1.c4	e6
2.e4	b6
3.d4	Bb7
4.Nc3	Bb4
5.Qc2	Qh4!?

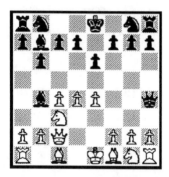

This is what was meant earlier when we talked about unusual Queen moves after 1.d4. On h4, the Queen pressures the e4-pawn and prevents its defense by f2-f3.

6.Bd3	f5

Another key element in Black's attack on the center. Black exploits White's legal inability to play 7.f3 and his tactical inability to play 7.exf5 (7...Bxg2).

7.g3	Qe7
8.f3	Nf6
9.Bg5	

This is not a piece White wanted to trade off but he saw no easier defense of the threatened e-pawn. After 9.exf5 exf5+ 10.Kf2 0-0 Black has excellent play.

9...	h6
10.Bxf6	Qxf6
11.Nge2	Nc6!

Blocking the c-pawn this way is another common feature of 1.d4 b6 games. Black is transferring the attack from e4 to d4 now that White has traded off his good defensive Bishop.

12.a3	Be7
13.e5	

Giving Black a tactical opportunity.

13...	Nxd4!
14.exf6?!	

Accepting the piece sacrifice the other way – 14.Nxd4 Qxe5 + 15.Nde2 Bxf3 – was probably better.

14...	Nxc2 +
15.Bxc2	Bxf6
16.Kf2	g5

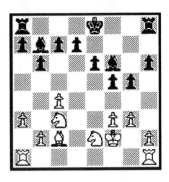

Black only has two pawns for the piece but his Bishops work well with his plan of advancing Kingside.

17.Rhe1	0-0-0
18.Rad1	h5
19.Nc1?!	g4!
20.f4	h4

White's inability to challenge the h-file with Rh1 now begins to hurt him.

21.Rd2	hxg3 +
22.hxg3	Rh2 +

23.Ke3	Rh3
24.Rg1	c5

Setting up an immediate threat of ...Bd4+ and preparing to push the d-pawn.

25.N1e2	Rh5
26.Ba4	d5
27.cxd5	exd5
28.Kd3?	d4!

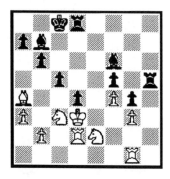

Now the pawns, supported by the Bishops, complete a rout.

29.Nd1	Ba6+
30.Kc2	d3+
31.Kc1	dxe2
32.Rxd8+	Kxd8
33.Nc3	Bd4!

It's not just that the Black d-pawn has won back a piece: it is also threatening to advance to the first rank with the help of ...Bf2.

34.Re1	Bf2
35.Rxe2	Bxe2
36.Nxe2	Ke7

There are several ways of winning this now.

37.Bc6	Rh6

38.Bb7	Rd6
39.Kc2	Be1
40.Ba6	Rd8
41.b3	Kd6
42.a4!	

White has stopped the queenside pawn from advancing and Black is still looking for a way for his Rook to penetrate effectively.

42...	Kc6
43.Bc4	Rd2+
44.Kc1	Rd8
45.Kc2	Rh8
46.Be6	Re8
47.Bc4	Re3!

This wins the g-pawn and ends resistance quickly. Black can even afford to sacrifice the Exchange for the two kingside pawns.

48.Bd3	Kd6
49.Bc4	Bxg3
50.Kd2	Rxe2+!

Bishops-of-opposite-color endings are not drawish when you're three pawns up.

51.Kxe2	Bxf4

White resigns

There are a number of other themes – both tactical and positional – in the 1...b6 system. They will be explored in the ensuing eight chapters. We'll consider 1...b6 in this order:

Chapter One: White plays 1.e4 and the natural 3.Nc3.
Chapter Two: White plays 1.e4 / 3.Bd3
Chapter Three: The main 1.e4 line
Chapter Four: White begins with 1.d4
Chapter Five: White blocks with 3.d5
Chapter Six: White accepts the 3.e4 challenge
Chapter Seven: The main 1.d4 line
Chapter Eight: White delays d2-d4

Chapter One
White Plays the Natural 3.Nc3

1.e4   b6

In the very early days of 1...b6, White often tried something like 2.Bc4 or 2.g3 or 2.Nf3. Such supercautious strategies allow Black to obtain a pleasant version of a closed Sicilian Defense when he plays ...c7-c5.

For example, 2.Nf3 Bb7 3.Nc3 e6 4.a3?! c5 5.Be2 Be7 6.d3 Nf6 and in Green-Owen, London 1862 Black stood quite well following 7.e5 Nd5 8.Nxd5 Bxd5 9.c4 Bb7 10.0-0 0-0 and 11...Nc6.

2.d4

Too much timidity by White will encourage Black to consider his own advances in the center. For example, 2.Nf3 Bb7 3.d3 – intending to play the opening like a King's Indian Reversed – allows Black to seize the initiative with 3...d5!.

Then 4.exd5 Qxd5! 5.Nc3 Qe6+ 6.Be3 Nf6 gives Black somewhat superior chances in the center (7.Be2 g6 8.0-0 Bg7 9.Re1 0-0 and 10...c5 in Zuckerman-Soltis, New York 1977).

2...   Bb7
3.Nc3

This is the move your fingers tell you to make: "Knights before Bishops," as the old saying goes.

But instinct often betrays players in the opening. That's one of the main reasons players choose 1...b6 from time to time. Natural moves don't necessarily work against it. The Knight move now encourages Black into setting up an annoying ...Bb4 pin.

3...   e6

(see diagram next page)

Preparing 4...Bb4. Here we have a wide choice of moves at White's disposal. We will examine: (a) The "Austrian" 4.f4, (b) The Counter-fianchetto, 4.g3, (c) The Developing 4.Nf3, (d) The Blocking 4.d5, (e) The Prophylactic 4.a3, and finally (f) 4.Bd3

(a)
The "Austrian" 4.f4

4.f4

This would be the "Austrian Attack" – if this were the Pirc Defense. Here, however, White does not need this over-protection of e5 and there's nothing Austrian about the position at all. In fact, White might do better to keep the f-pawn in reserve in case he needs to advance it only to f3, reinforcing his e4-pawn.

4...   Bb4!

Of course. Black's plan is to provoke White into advancing the e-pawn, thereby opening the diagonal of the b7-Bishop. Now the ugly 5.e5?! could be well handled by 5...c5 or 5...Ne7.

5.Bd3

There is no other convenient method of defending the e4-pawn because 5.d5 allows the pressure of 5...Nf6 and 5.Qf3 walks into a pin (5.Qf3 Nf6 6.Bd3 c5 7.Ne2 c4!? 8.Bxc4 Bxe4).

5...   Nf6
6.Qe2

Again, White does not have wide latitude in the defense of his center. After 6.Bd2 d5! Black equalizes fairly quickly: 7.e5 Bxc3 8.Bxc3 Ne4 or 7.exd5 Nxd5 8.Nxd5 Bxd2 + 9.Qxd2 Qxd5 (Ramos-Kapitaniak, corr. 1980 continued 10.Nf3 Nd7 11.c4 Qh5 12.Ne5 Nxe5, etc.).

6...   d5
7.e5?!

Inconsistent with his fourth move is the exchange of pawns on d5 – yet that may be best. After 7.dxe5 Nxd5 Black has no problems and *ECO* calls this position equal. Actually, some defenders will prefer Black following 8.Bd2 Nxc3 9.bxc3 Be7 10.Nf3 0-0 11.0-0 c5 and 12...Nc6.

7...   Ne4
8.Bd2   Bxc3

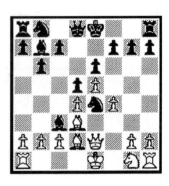

And after 9...Qh4+ Black holds an obvious edge (10.g3 Nxg3 11.Qf2 Nf5).

(b)
The Counter-fianchetto 4.g3
(after 1.e4 b6 2.d4 Bb7 3.Nc3 e6)
4.g3

Answering ...Bb7 with Bg2 makes some sense but it also invites an immediate tactical annoyance.

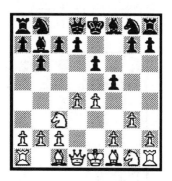

4...   f5!?

Usually this flanking attack on the center will be seen in variations that begin with 1.d4 or 1.c4. Here, however, it commands White's attention to the defense of e4 (5.exf5?? Bxh1).

5.Bg2

One of the few games in this line to emerge from the 1...b6 archives goes 5...Nf6 6.Bg5! Be7 7.Bxf6 Bxf6 8.Nge2 and White had a quite pleasant game (Lundgren-Nordstrom, corr. 1974).

5...   Bb4

The White center faces some difficulties. After 6.d5 Black can follow with 6...Nf6 (7.Bg5 h6 8.Bxf6 Qxf6, or 7.dxe6 Nxe4 8.Qd4 Qe7, or 7.exf5 0-0!?).

(c)
The Developing 4.Nf3
(after 1.e4 b6 2.d4 Bb7 3.Nc3 e6)
4.Nf3

Bringing out the second Knight is so natural that this is one of the positions you will almost certainly encounter. For this reason, it deserves a harder look.

4...   Bb4

Once again Black exploits the pinning problems White now faces.

5.Bd3

White is in a better position to push a pawn here but 5.e5 or 5.d5 are both somewhat innocuous after 5...Ne7, e.g. 5.e5 Ne7 6.Bd3 d6 7.Bf4 Ng6.

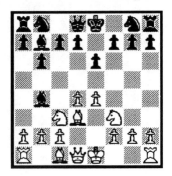

5...   Nf6

Black usually delays this natural move in the 1...b6 system. Sometimes he does it to retain the possibility of ...f7-f5 or ...Ne7 or even ...Nh6. And other times he delays it until he can find a square for his Knight if it is attacked by e4-e5.

6.Bg5!

This appears best. After 6.e5 Ne4 7.Bd2 Black can obtain good play with either 7...Nxd2 8.Qxd2 d6 or 8...Bxf3 9.gxf3 Nc6 as we'll see in section (f) below.

The gambit line 6.e5 Ne4 7.0-0!? resembles a notorious variation of the Nimzo-Indian. After 7...Nxc3 8.bxc3 Bxc3 9.Rb1 White has some chances

(9...Nc6 10.Bg5 Ne7 11.Rb3 Ba5 12.c4 h6 13.Bc1! as in Faas-Turikov, Leningrad 1975-76).

But Black improves with 10...f6 and ...Qe7, e.g. 11.exf6 gxf6 12.Ne5?! Nxe5 13.dxe5 Bxe5 14.Qh5+ Ke7 or 12.Bh4 Qe7 13.d5 exd5 14.Rb3 Ba5.

6...   **h6**

Black should act to break the pin and stop 7.e5. Now on 7.Bh4 Black wins material safely with 7...g5 8.Nxg5 hxg5 9.Bxg5 Rg8 10.h4 Be7.

7.Bxf6   **Qxf6**

8.0-0

It would be premature to advance here with 8.e5 since after 8...Qf4! Black's Queen is not easily driven from its powerful perch. Then 9.Qe2 Bxf3 10.Qxf3 Qxf3 11.gxf3 Nc6 12.Be4 is OK for White but 9...Nc6 looks preferable.

8...   **Bxc3**

Black wants to build a pawn structure on dark squares but wanted to avoid 8...d6 9.e5 dxe5 10.Ne4!?.

9.bxc3   **d6**

Black, naturally, positions his pawn on dark squares now that the Bishops that guard them are gone.

10.Nd2!

This appears much better than 10.a4 0-0 11.a5 which lead to a closed and dead even middlegame in Liberzon-Larsen, Geneva 1977 after 11...e5 12.Qe2 Nc6 13.a6 Bc8 14.d5 Ne7 and ...Ng6-f4.

10...   **e5**

More adventurous players will try 10...g5, ...Nc6 and eventually ...0-0-0.

11.f4!

Again the strongest. White forces the opening of lines for his better developed pieces. If, instead, the positional horror 11.d5 0-0 and ...Nd7-c5 favors the superior Bishop and pawns.

If White is going to sacrifice, this is better than the delayed 11.Nb3 Nc6 12. f4 because then 12...exf4 and ...Ne7-g6 offers Black a pleasant middlegame.

11...   **exd4**

12.e5

Again there is scant choice if White is serious about obtaining compensation.

12...	**dxe5**

13.Qh5

Perhaps 13.fxe5 Qg5 (not 13...Qxe5?? 14.Re1) 14.Nf3 is better. After 14...Qe3+ 15.Kh1 0-0 16.cxd4 (Dautov-Kengis, Daugavpils 1989) White has a slight edge that Black can contain with 16...Nd7.

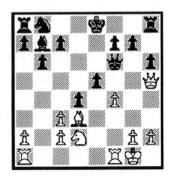

This is a critical position since 13...0-0 14. fxe5 Qg5 15.Qxg5 is known to favor White.

13...	**g6!**

14.Qh3

Better than 14.Qe2 Nc6! which favored Black in Ionescu-Smyslov, Sochi 1986. See Illustrative Game 1.

14...	**exf4!**
15.Rae1 +	**Kf8**

White has compensation for his pawns but Black should be safe enough following 16.Ne4 Qe5 and then ...Kg7 and ...Nc6.

(d)
The Blocking 4.d5
(after 1.e4 b6 2.d4 Bb7 3.Nc3 e6)
4.d5

Driving the d-pawn forward can be an effective strategy for White – provided he can maintain the pawn at d5. This is easier to do after 1.d4 and 2.c4 as we'll see in Chapter Five.

4...   Nf6

The immediate 4...Bb4 may also work well since 5.Qd4 invites 5...Bxc3 + 6.Qxc3 Nf6. And if 7.Bg5, then perhaps 7...exd5 8.e5 d4!? (9.Qxd4 Nc6 and 10...Qe7).

5.Bg5

Since 5.dxe6 fxe6 acknowledges that something has gone wrong in White's plan (6.e5 Nd5 is at least equal), White should try to maintain the d5-pawn with this pinning or 5.a3.

The prophylactic 5.a3 deserves some testing, which it has not had yet. Black seems to be doing well after 5...exd5 6.exd5 Bc5 (and 7...Qe7 +) but it is hard to tell.

5...   Bb4!?

There isn't anything wrong with 5...Be7, which threatens both 6...Nxd5 and 6...Nxe4, or 5...h6 6.Bh4 Be7.

The text, with its threat of 6...h6 7.Bh4 g5 and 8...Nxe4 is not easily met.

6.Qd4

This doesn't work. White may not be confident about 6.e5 h6 7.Bh4 g5 or 7.exf6 hxg5 8.fxg7 Rg8 9.dxe6 Qe7!? but the text is based on a tactical oversight.

6...   Bxc3 +

7.Qxc3

7...   Nxe4!

Black is fully equal after 8.Bxd8 Nxc3 and then 9.Bxc7 Nxd5. A major mistake for White is the appealing 8.Qxg7? because after 8...Qxg5 9.Qxh8+ Ke7 Black has a terrific initiative (10.Rd1 exd5 11.Qxh7 Nc6 12.Nf3 Qf6 13.Rxd5 Re8 and Black won in Ruppelt-Rellstab, Wedel 1977 after 14.Qh4 Kd8 15.Qg4 Ne5!).

(e)
The Prophylactic 4.a3
(after 1.e4 b6 2.d4 Bb7 3.Nc3 e6)
4.a3

This super-cautious move, which Tigran Petrosian brought into respectability in Queenside openings, also seems appropriate in this line. Yet it has never gained much attention, perhaps because players who open 1.e4 can't bring themselves to move the a-pawn this early in the game.

4...   Nf6

Black takes the opportunity to pressure e4 and awaits events.

5.Bd3

On 5.e5 the Knight heads into d5. Then 6.Nxd5 Bxd5 7.c4 Bb7 8.d5 looks impressive but Black can fight back with 8...Qe7 and 9...d6.

5...   c5!

When White is not able to respond d4-d5, this is generally a good way of reaching a version of the Sicilian Defense.

6.Nf3

In comparable positions of Chapter Three, White (with Nf3 instead of Nc3) can play c2-c3. Here he can't.

6...   cxd4!

Much better than the tempting 6...c4 7.Bxc4 Nxe4 8.Nxe4 Bxe4 9.Qe2 which gives White too much of an initiative in the center.

7.Nxd4   Nc6

All of White's moves are useful in the Sicilian Defense. But so are Black's. After 8.Nb3 Be7 9.f4 d6 10.0-0 0-0 11.Be3 a6, or 8.Be3 Bc5 9.Nxc6 Bxc6 10.Bxc5 bxc5 the usual Sicilian complications should keep matters double-edged and relatively equal.

(f)
4.Bd3
(after 1.e4 b6 2.d4 Bb7 3.Nc3 e6)
4.Bd3

This is the most popular move in the position, a piece-developer that protects the chief target in the center.

4...   Bb4

5.Nf3

There are other playable developing moves, such as 5.Qe2 and then 5...Nf6 6.Nf3 reaches the main line. Wildly aggressive ideas such as 5.Qg4? only lead to trouble after 5...Nf6! 6.Qxg7 Rg8.

But there is independent value in 5.Nge2. Then 5...Nf6 6.a3 favors White, since he gets the two-Bishop advantage without cost. Better is 5...c5, striking at the center before White can support d4-d5.

Then after 6.0-0 cxd4 7.Nxd4 Nc6 Black reaches a position similar to the one considered in (e) and elsewhere. The real test of 5...c5 is probably 6.a3 (and if 6...Bxc3+ then 7.Nxc3 cxd4 8.Nb5). However, 6...Ba5 looks adequate.

5...   Nf6

6.Qe2

With 6.Bg5 we are right back in the position examined in some detail in (d) above. The text is a more natural – what the Russians call "more principled" – method of meeting the threat to e4.

6...   d5!

A well timed advance. Now 7.exd5 Qxd5 makes the b7-Bishop useful. For example, 8.Bd2 Bxc3 9.Bxc3 Nbd7 10.0-0 Ne4 eliminates all dangers in the position (11.Bxe4 Qxe4 12.Qxe4 Bxe4 13.Ne1 Nf6 and 14...0-0-0 as in Mikhalschishin-Gurgenidze, USSR 1981).

But more enterprising is 7...Nxd5 and 8...Nxc3, followed by attacking the center with ...c7-c5. See Illustrative Game 2 for a particularly impressive example of Black's opportunities.

7.e5   Ne4

Of course. The Knight stands much better here than on d7.

Now 8.Bxe4 dxe4 makes the d4-pawn as weak as the newly created e4-pawn.

8.Bd2

Here 8.0-0!? Nxc3 9.bxc3 Bxc3 comes to mind. But 8...Bxc3! 9.bxc3 Nxc3 turns out to be superior. See the note to White's seventh move in Illustrative Game 2.

8...   Bxc3
9.bxc3

Now 9...f5 would anchor the Knight in the center and prepare Black's assault on the Queenside with ...Nc6-a5 and ...c7-c5. But White plays 10.exf6 gxf6 11.c4 with dangerous open lines.

9...   Nc6!?

An untried gambit, seeking control of the light squares after 10.Bxe4 dxe4 11.Qxe4 Na5 12.Qe2 Bd5. He should then have excellent compensation when you consider the two Bishops (the finesse 11.Ng5, rather than 11.Qxe4, invites 11...Qd5 or 11...Na5 12.Nxe4 Qd5).

Illustrative Games

(1) Ionescu-Smyslov, Sochi 1986

1.Nf3   b6

2.e4

White evidently had doubts about his chances in the quiet systems introduced by 2.c4 Bb7 3.Nc3. We'll consider such positions in Chapter Eight.

2...   Bb7

3.Nc3   e6

4.d4

Accepting the pin. After 4.a3 Black has a choice between 4...c5, an invitation to a Sicilian Defense, or 4...Nf6 5.e5 Nd5.

4...	Bb4!
5.Bd3	Nf6
6.Bg5	

White adopts the dangerous attacking plan examined in (c) above.

6...	h6
7.Bxf6	Qxf6
8.0-0	Bxc3
9.bxc3	d6
10.Nd2	

Unexplored here is the quieter defense, with 10...Nc6 11.f4 Qd8.

10...	e5
11.f4!	exd4
12.e5	dxe5
13.Qh5	g6

Naturally, 14.Qxe5 + ? Qxe5 15.fxe5 helps Black by killing the attack before White can justify his sacrifices.

14.Qe2	Nc6!

Black desperately needs development and this Knight arrives just in time. Now 15.f5 g5 16.Ne4 Qd8 offers compensation for a pawn. But White is down two pawns.

15.fxe5	**Qe7**
16.e6	**f5!**

Another good decision. Black can get Queens off the board with 16...Qxe6 17.Qxe6+ fxe6 but 18.Bxg6+ Kd8 19.Rf6 gives White good compensation.

17.Nb3	**0-0-0!**
18.cxd4	**Nxd4**
19.Nxd4	**Rxd4**
20.Qe5?!	

Now Black begins a precipitous decline. With 20...Qc5! he would establish a winning endgame (because 21.Qxh8+ allows 21...Rd8+).

20...	**Rhd8**
21.Rae1	**Ra4?**

A second error: Black should take precautions with 21...Kb8.

22.Bb5!	**Rxa2?**
23.Rd1!	

A complete turnaround has occurred, with Rd7 or Rxd8+ threatened. Now 23...Rg8 24.Rd7 Qc5+ leads to a lost ending following 25.Qxc5 bxc5 26.e7 Ba6 27.Rfd1 and 28.Rd8.

23...	**Rxc2**

24.Rxd8+	**Qxd8**

Forced, because of 24...Kxd8? 25.Qh8+.

25.Bd7+	**Kb8**
26.Rd1	**Qg8!?**

The threat was to Queen the pawn with 27.e7. The winner pointed out later that 26...Rxg2+ 27.Kf1 Qh4 allows 28.Qh8+ and wins. After the text, however, 27.e7 loses to 27...Rxg2+ 28.Kf1 Qc4+!.

27.Bb5!	**a6**
28.e7	**Rxg2+**
29.Kf1	**Qb3!?**
30.e8=Q+	

The game continues only because of momentum and the illusion of counterplay from ...Qf3+ or ...Qh3.

30...	**Ka7**
31.Be2!	**Qh3**
32.Ke1!	**Qh4+**
33.Kd2	**Qg5+**
34.Kc3!	**Black resigns**

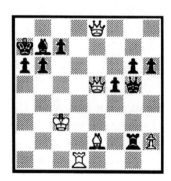

(2) Mortesen-Keene, Arhus 1976

1.Nf3	**b6**
2.e4	

Because of the generally poor reputation of 1...b6 before 1980 – and even in our time – players tended in 1976 to shift the opening into 1.e4 positions rather than keeping it closed with 2.c4.

2...	**Bb7**
3.Nc3	**e6**
4.d4	**Bb4**
5.Bd3	**Nf6**
6.Qe2	**d5**
7.exd5	

This is a natural reaction, opening lines for White's slightly more advanced development. But 7.e5 may test Black more.

7...	**Nxd5**
8.Bd2	

In another game from this tournament (Rosell-Keene, Arhus 1976) White ventured the 8.0-0 gambit. Black accepted it with 8...Bxc3! 9.bxc3 Nxc3, a good plan considering that the attacked Queen has no good escape square and therefore Black gains valuable time to castle.

Before the c1-Bishop could enter the game, Black repelled the enemy Queen with 10.Qe5 0-0 (intending 11...Nd7) 11.Qh5 g6 12.Qh3.

There followed 12...Nd7 13.Re1 c5 14.dxc5? Nxc5, after which Black took complete control and was soon winning (15.Ng5 h5 16.Bf4 Nxd3 17.cxd3 Qf6 18.Be5 Qxg5 19.Bxc3 Rac8 20.Re5 Bxg2!!).

8...	**Nxc3**
9.bxc3	

A fairly automatic recapture since it gains time and keeps Black's pieces a bit congested. After 9.Bxc3 Bxc3+ 10.bxc3 0-0 11.0-0 c5 or 11...Nd7 Black's counterplay should at least balance White's edge in space and development.

9...	**Be7**
10.0-0	**0-0**
11.Rad1	

White's attack may be repulsed but it cannot be safely ignored .

11...	**Nd7**
12.Bf4	**Nf6**
13.c4	

Suspicious. This deprives Black of d5 (13.Ne5 Qd5) but weakens d4 considerably.

| **13...** | **c5!** |

A good (perhaps temporary) sacrifice of a pawn which cripples White's center.

| **14.dxc5** | **Qe8** |

Of course, not 14...Bxc5 15.Bxh7 + and 16.Rxd8.

| **15.cxb6** | **axb6** |
| **16.Ne5** | |

Trying to hold the a-pawn with 16.Ra1 Ra4 and ...Qa8 was probably doomed.

16...	**Rxa2**
17.Bg5	**Kh8**
18.Qe3	**Ra5!**
19.Bxf6	

Other moves (19.Rfe1, 19.Qh3) allow a strong 19...Ne4.

| **19...** | **Bxf6** |
| **20.Qxb6?** | |

White can fight on with 20.Qh3 h6 21.Ng4 but the text loses quickly.

20...	Qa8!
21.Nd7	Bxg2

The triumph of Black's strategy on the a8-g2 diagonal.

22.Nxf8	Rg5!

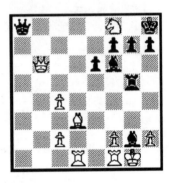

23.f4

This is hopeless since 23...Bxf1 + 24.fxg5 allows mate on g2.

23...	Bxf1 +
24.Kxf1	Qg2 +
25.Ke1	Re5 + !

Forcing mate. All in all, a very impressive little game.

26.fxe5	Bh4 +
27.Qf2	Qxf2 Mate

Chapter Two
White Plays 3.Bd3

Since there are some obvious problems arising out of Nc3/...Bb4, in this chapter we will consider development systems by White in which he avoids the Bishop pin.

1.e4   b6

The London 1899 tournament book commented, "It is nothing new to say that the Fianchetto is not considered a good defense. White has only...to establish a well-supported center, and so keep Black's Bishops inactive."

Keeping them inactive was easier in 1899 than today.

2.d4   Bb7
3.Bd3

The advantages of this defense of the e-pawn – over 3.Nc3 – were known back in the 1850's

Note that 3.Nd2 may also be played, with likely transposition into the next chapter after 3...e6 4.Ngf3 c5 5.c3 Nf6.

3...   e6

Naturally Black avoids the ancient attempt at suicide 3...f5??, which allows 4.exf5 Bxg2? 5.Qh5 + .

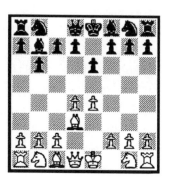

Black's pinning plan of the last chapter will not be readily available. But he has other strategies, including the attack on d4 with ...c7-c5 with ...Nc6 and the pressuring of e4 with ...Nf6 and ...d5.

From White's point of view, another huge choice arises here. He can decide from among: (a) 4.Ne2, (b) 4.Nh3, (c) 4.f4, (d) 4.c3, (e) 4.Be3, (f) 4.Qe2, (g) 4.c4 and finally the main line: 4.Nf3, which we'll consider in the next chapter.

(a)
4.Ne2
(after 1.e4 b6 2.d4 Bb7 3.Bd3 e6)
4.Ne2

This conservative Knight move keeps White's f-pawn free to advance. It occurred in one of the very first 1...b6 games, Lichtenhein-Perrin, New York 1857 and led to a smashing victory after 4...g6 5.0-0 Bg7 6.c3 Ne7 7.f4 f5? 8.e5 d6 9.Nd2 dxe5 10.fxe5 Bxe5? 11.Bc4 Bd6 12.Bxe6.

The problem with 4.Ne2 is that the Knight is not particularly well placed either on e2 or g3, where it may be needed to defend e4.

4...   c5

Usually after White has blocked his access to d5 and cannot support an advance of his d-pawn, Black will break in the center with ...c7-c5.

5.c3

"Sicilianizing" the opening, with 4.Nbc3 for example, is not a problem for Black, as we noted in the last chapter after 4...cxd4 5.Nxd4 Nc6.

5...   Nf6

Now 6.Ng3 solves one central problem but after 6...cxd4 7.cxd4 Nc6 Black points out another, newly created one (8.Bc2 or 8.Be3 allow 8...Nb4).

6.Nd2

One reason for this move is to clear a retreat line for the Bishop, in anticipation of the aforementioned 6...cxd4 7.cxd4 Nb4.

Also, note that 6.e5 Nd5 gives Black an excellent Knight outpost and an easier opening than White wants to grant him.

6...   Nc6

7.a3

A normal precaution against the ...cxd4/...Nb4 idea. White can delay this for a while (7.0-0 cxd4 8.cxd4 Nb4 9.Bb1 and if 9...Ba6, then 10.Re1 Nd3 11.Bxd3 Bxd3 12.Nc3 with a nice lead in development).

7... d6

This cautious approach appears to be best. Black will fianchetto his other Bishop and await events in the center.

8.0-0 g6
9.h3 Bg7

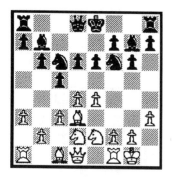

For example, 10.b4 0-0 11.Rb1 Ne7! is a good waiting policy, stopping any dangerous central advance and waiting until Black's heavy pieces are in play.

This occurred in Marjanovich-Sahovic, Bled 1979 and led to balanced play after the opening of the c-file (12.Re1 cxd4 13.cxd4 Qd7 and ...Rac8).

(b)
4.Nh3
(after 1.e4 b6 2.d4 Bb7 3.Bd3 e6)
4.Nh3

This was Mikhail Tchigorin's choice back in the 1890's – although it was being given a question mark 40 years before. The "Knight-on-the-rim" move was also tried on occasion by Paul Morphy but has gained little respectability since. The Knight loses contact with the center here and allows Black a natural challenge:

4...   c5!

White's inability to play Nf3 or Ne2 costs him here. Now 5.c3 would be met by 5...Nc6 6.Be3 Nf6 7.0-0 cxd4 8.cxd4 Nb4!.

In fact, in Hampton-Owen, Birmingham 1858 (!) Black equalized by way of 9.f3 Nxd3 10.Qxd3 Be7 11.Nc3 0-0 12.Rad1 and now 12...Ne8!? followed by 13...Nd6 and 14...f5.

5.dxc5!?

Opening the center – in fact, accepting a somewhat dubious version of the Sicilian Defense – does not seem right here, despite Tchigorin's success with it.

5...   Bxc5
6.0-0   Nf6

7.Nc3   Nc6
8.Bf4

The Bishop occupies the best square needed for the exiled h3-Knight's reemergence. But 8.Nf4 0-0 9.Re1 Ne5 or 8.Kh1 0-0 9.f4 d6 10.Ng5 e5 aren't particularly impressive alternatives for White.

In Tchigorin-Tinsley, London 1899 Black went off on his own tangent with 8...Nb4? but after 9.e5 Nxd3 10.Qxd3 Nd5 11.Nxd5 Bxd5 12.Qg3 he marred a good position with 12...Kf8? instead of 12...Bf8.

8...   d6

Now with ...0-0 and ...Rc8/...Ne5 Black should achieve a fine position. He may even play the position like a Sveshnikov Sicilian with ...e6-e5 and if Bg5, then ...Ne7.

(c)
4.f4
(after 1.e4 b6 2.d4 Bb7 3.Bd3 e6)
4.f4

Why misplace the Knight on h3 in order to free the f-pawn when you can play this move immediately? That was the argument in favor of 4.f4 over 4.Nh3.

Note that 4.f3, adding protection to e4, is unnecessary and encourages Black to open the g1-a7 diagonal with 4...c5. Then 5.c3 Nc6 6.Ne2 allows another version of the maneuver that John Owen made famous: 6...cxd4 7.cxd4 Nb4!.

4...   c5!

Note that Black should avoid this move when White can respond d4-d5 (that is, before Black has played ...e7-e6 and before White has played Bd3).

5.c3   Nf6
6.Qe2

Advancing to e5 is particularly risky when White has created a hole at e3 (6.e5 Nd5 7.Be4? Ne3, or 7.Nd2? Ne3).

6...   cxd4
7.cxd4   Nc6

(see next diagram)

Once again Owen's maneuver brings a pleasant result. Now 8.Nf3 Nb4 9.Nc3 Nxd3+ 10.Qxd3 Bb4 11.Nd2 0-0 should give Black reasonable chances. The fact that White has allowed the exchange of his good Bishop is bound to cost him in the middlegame.There hasn't been much experience with this position since Barnes-Owen, London 1862 - and that game went 12.0-0 Rc8 13.e5 Nd5 14.Nde4 f5!? with equal play. Better for Black is 14...Nxc3 15.Nxc3 Qc7 (16.Bd2 Qc4 or 16.Ne4 Qc2).

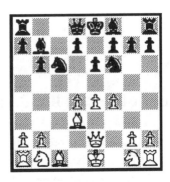

(d)
4.c3
(after 1.e4 b6 2.d4 Bb7 3.Bd3 e6)
4.c3

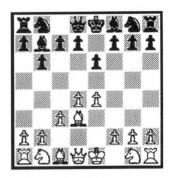

This is basically a waiting move. White voluntarily gives up the option of Nc3 because he knows that he doesn't want to be pinned by ...Bb4. He also knows that his center will be attacked by 4...c5, so he takes the usual safeguards before rather than after that advance.

4...	**c5**

With this we transpose into the next chapter (5.Nf3 Nf6 6.Nbd2 Be7 or 6.e5 Nd5).

(e)
4.Be3
(after 1.e4 b6 2.d4 Bb7 3.Bd3 e6)
4.Be3

One of the misleading aspects of studying chess openings is that you often encounter a lot of past master experience involving an essentially poor move. This usually happens because some questionable idea scored a few successes half a century ago and was copied in the games of lesser players.

In the case of 4.Be3, its successes were not half a century, but a full century ago. Although it was used by players such as David Janowsky, Joseph Blackburne and George MacKenzie, the Bishop move is unlikely to make a modern player worry.

4...	**Nf6**

This is useful since White does not have the usual defense of the e-pawn with 5.Qe2 because the Bishop interferes. Also, if the White e-pawn ever advances, a Black Knight will stand well on d5, where it attacks e3.

5.Nc3

White's development makes a clumsier than usual impression after 5.Nd2 c5 6.c3 Nc6 7.Ngf3 cxd4 8.cxd4 Nb4 9.Bb1 Ba6 although 7.a3! Be7 8.Ngf3 0-0 9.0-0 Rc8 is nothing much for either side.

Worse is 6.dxc5 Bxc5 7.Bxc5 bxc5 8.Ne2 0-0 9.0-0 Nc6, with at least equality as in an old game of Owen's.

5...	**Bb4**

Black returns to the strategy of the previous chapter – simply because White allows it. Here 5...c5 would have been a perfectly reasonable alternative.

6.f3

There was not much of a choice (6.Bg5 h6; 6.e5? Bxg2; 6.Qf3!? c5 7.Nge2 c4).

6...   0-0

Here 6...c5 or 6...d5 7.e5 Nfd7 and 8...c5 come to mind.

7.Nge2   c5

Now Lowenthal-Owen, London 1866 went 8.dxc5?! bxc5 9.0-0 Bxc3? 10.Nxc3 Qa5 11.e5!, after which White got the upper hand. Better was 8...Bxc5! to weaken the dark squares.

A more modern handling of the position would be 8.0-0 cxd4 9.Nxd4 Nc6 with a reasonable Sicilian Defense.

(f)
4.Qe2
(after 1.e4 b6 2.d4 Bb7 3.Bd3 e6)
4.Qe2

This was employed twice by S.S. Boden in his 1858 match with the Rev. Owen. Since Owen met the Queen move once each with 4...Be7 and 4...g6, the idea was not seriously tested for some time.

4...   Nf6

Black shouldn't fear 4...c5 because of 5.d5, since 5...exd5 6.exd5 + Qe7 is hardly an endgame to dread. This may be Black's best move inasmuch as it avoids the complication from 5.c4 in our main line.

After 4...c5 5.c3 cxd4 6.cxd4 Nc6 the Owen maneuver is working again (7.Nf3 Nb4 8.Bc4 Rc8!).

5.c4!?

After 5.Nc3 Bb4 or 5.Nf3 c5 we reach more familiar positions. The text is an attempt to reach a 1.d4 b6 position but with none of Black's usual pressure on e4 to distract White.

5...   Bb4 +

As we'll see in Chapter Six, this effective check tends to ease Black's game and may enable him to build a favorable center on dark squares after a trade of Bishops.

6.Bd2

The problem for Black in this line is 6.Nc3!, after which he has a problem generating pressure in the center (no ...f5!).

6...   Bxd2 +
7.Nxd2   d6

Black intends to build a pawn center on dark squares as in a Bogo-Indian Defense.

For example, 8.Ngf3 Nc6 9.0-0 e5 10.d5 Nb4 11.Bb1 a5!. If White advances with 9.e5 dxe5 10.dxe5 Nd7 11.Bc2 Black continues 11...Qe7! followed by

Queenside castling (12.a3 a5! 13.0-0 g5 14.Ba4 0-0-0 15.Rfb1 Nc5 16.Bxc6 Bxc6 17.b4 Nd3 as in Kupreichik-Jacobsen, Copenhagen 1988).

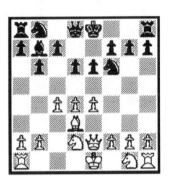

(g)
4.c4
(after 1.e4 b6 2.d4 Bb7 3.Bd3 e6)
4.c4

Taking advantage of his third move, White improves the size of his center. The most interesting reply is 4...f5 but the complications after 5.exf5 Bxg2 6.Qh5 + g6 7.fxg6 are probably too great for Black's health. Actually, we have transposed into a position usually reached by way of 1.d4 b6 2.c4 e6 3.e4 Bb7 4.Bd3. And for that reason we'll consider it in the place reserved for it, Chapter Six.

Chapter Three
The Main 1.e4 Line

The revival of 1...b6 began around 1976 – and lasted less than three years. While it remained in the repertoire of some masters as a weapon against 1.d4, it was soon discarded by those who had used it against 1.e4.

The reason is that by the end of the 1970's a "Main Line" had emerged – a main line that appeared to give White a clear advantage without having to take risks or make particularly committal moves. This main line, with 3.Bd3 e6 4.Nf3 c5 5.c3 is our concern in this chapter. Let's see what has happened since 1980.

1.e4	**b6**
2.d4	**Bb7**
3.Bd3	**e6**
4.Nf3	

White prepares quick Kingside castling – after which he may no longer be concerned about ...Bb4 and therefore can develop his b1-Knight at the more aggressive and ambitious square c3.

4...   **c5!**

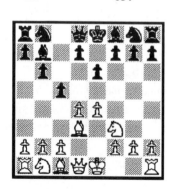

Taking advantage of White's current inability to play 5.d5. White has tried two basic approaches to 4...c5. He can allow a Sicilian Defense with (a) 5.0-0, or he can buttress his center with (b) 5.c3!.

(a)
"Sicilianizing" with 5.0-0
5.0-0

This colorless move leads directly into a Sicilian Defense with Black a bit more conservatively situated on the Queenside than with the usual ...a7-a6 and ...b7-b5.

The same thing results from 5.Nc3 cxd4 6.Nxd4 Nf6 7.0-0 Nc6 as in our line below – 8.Nxc6 dxc6!? 9.f4? Bc5 + 10.Kh1 h5! 11.Na4? Ng4! 12.Nxc5 Qh4 13.h3 Qg3! and Black was winning in Bogden-Lemachko, Gosa 1980.

5...   cxd4
6.Nxd4

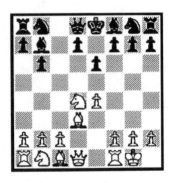

6...   Nc6

There is nothing particularly wrong with 6...d6, since 7.Bb5 + Nd7 8.Bc6 Bxc6 9.Nxc6 Qc7 leads to a typical Maroczy Bind position after the eventual c2-c4. Despite the exchange of light-squared Bishops, Black has a fine position (see Illustrative Game 4).

7.Nxc6

On 7.Nb3 Nf6 Black may be ready to push in the center: 8.Nc3 d5 9.exd5 Nxd5 or 8.c4 d6 9.Nc3 Be7 and later ...Nb4/...Nd7-c5.

7...   Bxc6

Recapturing with the pawn, as in the note to 5.0-0, makes more sense when White's Knight is already on c3. Here Black looks forward to pressuring the e4-pawn (perhaps even with ...Qc7-b7).

8.Nc3

The e-pawn may become a target for liquidation after 8.e5 Ne7, e.g. 9.Nd2 Qc7 10.Nf3 Ng6 and 11...d6.

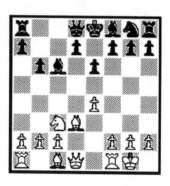

8...   d6

The situation is too early for 8...d5 9.e5 Ne7 10.f4 and later Ne2-d4.

9.Qe2   Be7

We are headed into a typical Sicilian Defense middlegame with two notable differences: Black's Queenside is less aggressively arranged than usual (no ...a7-a6 and ...b7-b5) while White has been lured into the usually disadvantageous exchange of Knights on c6.

The first factor helps White, the second helps Black. Chances should be roughly equal after, say, 10.b3 Nf6 11.Bb2 0-0 12.Rad1 Nd7.

(b)
5.c3
(after 1.e4 b6 2.d4 Bb7 3.Bd3 e6 4.Nf3 c5)
5.c3   Nf6

Now White usually defends the e-pawn with his Queen or Queen's Knight. We'll consider 6.Qe2 in (b2).

(b1)
6.Nbd2

White should probably resist the temptation to hit the f6-Knight because it simplifies Black's task in the center. For instance, 6.e5 Nd5 7.0-0 allows Black to obtain pleasant opportunities with 7...cxd4 8.cxd4 Nb4.

The more exact treatment by White is 7.a3! with play similar to Ristic-Nikolic, Smederevska Palanka 1982 (see Illustrative Game 6).

Note that 6.Bg5? is plainly out of place since Black can break the pin immediately with 6...h6. See Illustrative Game 7 for an ancient – but neatly handled – example of Black's play.

6...   Be7

In many cases Black should avoid – or at least delay – ...d7-d5, which reduces the position to a somewhat inferior French Defense when White responds e4-e5. Then Black no longer has d5 for his Knight and must retreat it to a square such as d7. See Illustrative Game 5 for a demonstration of the problems this poses for Black.

7.0-0

Also worth a try is 7.Qe2, protecting e4 as well as preventing Black from trading off Bishops with ...Ba6. After 7.0-0 cxd4 8.cxd4 Tony Miles has obtained good play with the 8...Ba6 idea. For example, 9.Bxa6 Nxa6 10.e5 Nd5 11.Ne4 leads to a position in which both players have a good Knight outpost in the center.

In Belotti-Miles, Forli 1991 Black's position appeared a bit loose after 11...0-0 12.Bg5! f6 13.exf6 gxf6 14.Bh6. But he soon obtained a good game with 14...Rf7 15.Rc1 Kh8 16.a3 Nac7 17.Nfd2 Qg8! and 18...Qg6.

7...	cxd4

8.cxd4

8...	d5

This is a rare case when offering a French Defense position turns out well for Black.

9.e5

White should avoid exchanges which free Black's game, e.g. 9.Qe2 dxe4 10.Nxe4 Nbd7 followed eventually by a double exchange of pieces on e4 and ...Nf6/...Qd5.

9...	Nfd7

Black will now exchange off his bad Bishop with ...Ba6 and mine the c-file. White cannot avoid the trade (10.Qe2 a5) and the blocking of the c-file will enable Black to equalize. For example, 10.a3 a5 11.Nb1 Ba6 12.Nc3 and before White gets to play 13.Nb5 Black has 12...Bxd3 13.Qxd3 Nc6 and ...Na7/...Rc8 with good

Queenside play, (e.g. 14.h4 Na7 15.Ng5 Rc8 as in Solomon-Miles, Australian Ch. 1992).

(b2)
6.Qe2
(after 1.e4 b6 2.d4 Bb7 3.Bd3 e6 4.Nf3 c5 5.c3 Nf6)
6.Qe2

This has also been played quite a bit but has suffered a recent setback thanks to Tony Miles.

6...	**Be7**
7.0-0	**Nc6**

This would be an appropriate point for White to expand, with 8.e5 Nd5 9.dxc5 bxc5 10.Na3 and 11.Nc4. However, 9...Bxc5 is much better.

White can also try 9.a3, intending 10.c4. But then 9...cxd4 10.cxd4 Na5! exploits the absence of the Queen from d1. And 10.c4?! Nc7 11.b4 allows Black an easy road to equality after 11...d6 12.exd6 Qxd6 13.Bb2 Bf6 14.Nbd2 Ne5 15.Be4 d3! (Sveshnikov-Osachuk, USSR 1981).

8.a3

This is the move that was thought to have refuted 1...b6 in the late 1970's. The b4 square is denied to Black while White gives himself a promising option of Queenside expansion with b2-b4.

8...	**Na5!**

This was the new move of Miles' that reinvigorated the 1...b6 opening. Before 1992, Black usually played quietly with moves such as 8...d6 and obtained a somewhat constricted game (9.b4!).

9.Nbd2

White simply cannot allow 9...Nb3.

9...   **c4!**

Black is perfectly willing to trade his c-pawn for the e-pawn (10.Nxc4 Nxc4 11.Bxc4 Bxe4).

10.Bc2   Qc7

In comparable positions, Black obtains a bad game if he relinquishes pressure on the center with ...c5-c4. Here, however, Black can exploit White's problem in getting his Queenside pieces into play.

11.Ne5   **b5**

12.f4   **0-0**

This is a crucial position as it comes about from logical play that previously had been endorsed by theory as leading to a White edge. After 13.Ng4 Nxg4 14.Qxg4 Miles has had two opportunities to play 14...Nb3! against fellow grandmasters.

Against Kiril Georgiev at Biel 1992 he found his way to active equality following 15.Rb1! Nxd2 16.Bxd2 Bxe4! 17.Bxe4 f5.

But when Josif Dorfman played 15.Bxb3? against the Englishman at Tilburg 1992, Black got the upper hand with 15...cxb3 16.f5 exf5!, e.g. 17.Rxf5 d5 or 17.exf5? Bd6 18.Ne4 Bxe4 19.Qxe4 Bxh2+ 20.Kh1 Rae8.

Illustrative Games

(3) Boyarinov-Kengis, Pushkinsky Gori 1980

1.e4	b6
2.d4	e6
3.Nf3	Bb7
4.Bd3	c5
5.0-0	

Here 5...Nf6 is also played.

5...	cxd4
6.Nxd4	d6
7.Bb5 +	

More of a test is 7.f4 Nf6 8.f5 since then 8...e5 is met by 9.Bb5 + Ke7 (9...Nd7 10.Ne6!) and now 10.Ne6 fxe6 11.fxe6 Qc8 12.Nc3 Qxe6 with insufficient compensation for White's piece (Maksimovic-Sahovic, Nis 1977).

7...	Nd7
8.Bc6	Bxc6
9.Nxc6	Qc7
10.Nd4	Ngf6
11.Qe2	

Black could now try to prevent the Maroczy Bind from being completed with 11...Rc8.

11...	**Be7**
12.c4!	**0-0**
13.Nc3	

Traditional Maroczy Bind policy: White prevents ...b6-b5 and ...d6-d5 and develops his plans slowly until a method of exploiting his spatial edge presents itself.

13...	**a6**
14.Be3	**Rfe8**
15.Rac1	**Qb7**

The Queen is well placed here, in the absence of a light-squared Bishop. Note that Black's Rook is on e8 just in case White allows him to open the e-file with f2-f4-f5 and ...exf5 – or just ...e6-e5 in answer to f2-f4.

16.Bg5	**Rac8**
17.Kh1	**h6**
18.Bd2	**Bf8**
19.f4	**e5!**

A thematic thrust by Black which both stops e4-e5 and also opens a line of attack on the e4-pawn.

20.Nf5	**exf4**
21.Rxf4	**b5!**

As so often happens when White defends his side of the Bind, this liberating break can be played as a sacrifice.

22.cxb5	**d5**

The point of Black's play. Now 23.bxa6 Qxb2 threatens both 24...Nxe4 and 24...d4.

23.Re1	**axb5**
24.Qf1?!	**dxe4**
25.Nxb5	**Re6**

White can't even claim a material advantage as compensation for his misplaced pieces. Black now prepares the advance of his strong passed pawn – and also protects the Kingside against sacrifices on g7 and h6.

26.Bc3	**Rce8**
27.Ne3	

Else 27...e3 and 28...e2.

27...	**Rb6**
28.a4	**Bc5**

Among Black's tactical ideas now are ...Bxe3 and ...Nd5.

29.Ng4	**Ree6!**
30.Nxf6 +	**Nxf6**
31.Qc4	**Rbc6!**

Now the advance of the e-pawn can no longer be prevented.

32.Qe2	**e3!**
33.Rf3	**Nd5**
34.Nd4	**Bxd4!**

Winning at least a pawn.

35.Bxd4	**Qb4**
36.Bc3	**Nxc3**
37.bxc3	**Rxc3**

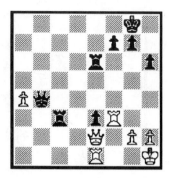

If White could somehow exchange the a-pawn for Black's e-pawn he would have excellent drawing chances. But that clearly is not possible and Black can win now by penetrating with his heavy pieces. He makes it look a little more difficult than it should be.

38.Qf1	Qe7?!
39.a5!	Ra3
40.Qb5	Qa7
41.Rf5	Ra2
42.h3	Qc7!

Black quickly spots the target square – g3 – created by White's last move.

43.Qd5	Qg3!

Now 44.Rff1 Rf2 is fairly hopeless so White pins his final hope on a pawn race.

44.Qxa2	Qxe1+
45.Kh2	e2
46.a6	Qd1
47.a7	e1 = Q

More exact was 47...Qd6 + first but it hardly matters now. Black's heavy pieces are overwhelming.

48.a8 = Q +	Kh7

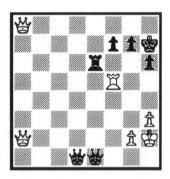

49.Qf2	Qh1 +
50.Kg3	Rg6 +
51.Kf4	Qh2 +

White resigns

(4) Matulovic-Sahovic, Bled 1984

1.e4	b6
2.d4	Bb7
3.Bd3	e6
4.Nf3	c5
5.c3	Nf6
6.Qe2	Be7
7.0-0	d5?

Even though Black can succeed in exchanging off his now-bad b7-Bishop, this leads to a dubious, constricted middlegame.

8.e5	Nfd7
9.a3	a5
10.a4!	

In contrast with positions in which White has spent a tempo on Nbd2, White can now occupy the newly-created hole at b5 in two Knight hops.

| 10... | Ba6 |

11.Na3!

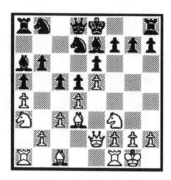

The Knight threatens to shut out the Bishop on b5. Later, it can shift to the Kingside, via c2 and e3.

11...	Bxd3
12.Qxd3	c4

This last move is a major decision. Black creates weaknesses at b3 as well as b6 and gives up the option of opening the c-file. As it stands, Black's only chances of favorably opening the position now stem from ...b6-b5 and ...f7-f6 – and neither look promising.

13.Qe2	Nc6
14.g3	0-0
15.h4	

White methodically prepares a Kingside attack with Ng5 and Qh5 or Qc2.

15...	Na7
16.Ng5!	Qe8
17.Re1	

Now 18.Qc2 is one idea and 18.Nc2 followed by Ne3-g4 is another. Black derives no benefit from 17...h6 because the Knight reemerges after 18.Nh3 and Nf4-h5.

17...	Bxg5
18.hxg5	

Another plan is visible: Kg2, Rh1 and Qh5.

18...	**Qe7**
19.Nc2	**b5**
20.Ne3!	**Qxg5**

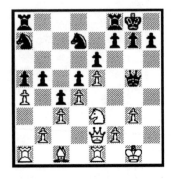

This seems foolhardy but 20...bxa4 allows 21.Ng4 followed by a dangerous attack via Kg2 and Rh1, or the sacrifice on f6.

21.Nxd5	**Qd8**
22.Ne3	**Nb6**
23.axb5	**Qc7**
24.Rxa5	

White is better on both wings. His fastest winning plan turns out to be the doubling of Rooks on the a-file.

24...	**Rfc8**
25.Bd2	**Rab8**
26.Rea1	**Rb7**
27.f4	**Qd7**
28.Qf3	

White's Bishop has become quite bad but there are too many other good things about his position. He now prepares f4-f5-f6, which cannot be stopped (28...g6? 29.Ng4).

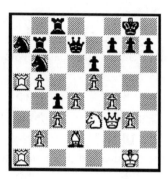

28...	Rcb8
29.f5	**Nxb5**
30.f6	**Nc7**
31.fxg7	**Nbd5**

This loses another pawn but 31...Ncd5 32.Ng4 would have set up a murderous check on h6.

32.Nxc4	**Ne8**
33.Bc1	**Qc7**
34.Rc5	**Qd7**
35.Nd2	**Black resigns**

White can win at his leisure with Ne4, Kg2 and c3-c4.

5) Ristic-Z.Nikolic, Smederevska Palanka 1982

1.e4	**b6**
2.d4	**Bb7**
3.Bd3	**e6**
4.Nf3	**Nf6**

Slightly inexact. Better is the immediate 4...c5, denying White the opportunity to push his center pawns as he does now.

5.e5	**Nd5**
6.a3	**c5**

7.c4!?	**Ne7**
8.dxc5	

Black was about to collapse the center anyway with 8...Nbc6 or 8...Bxf3/ 9...Nbc6.

8...	**bxc5**
9.0-0	**Ng6**
10.Nc3	**Nc6**

The e5-pawn can be defended two more times and attacked only once (11.Qe2 Qb8 12.Re1) but White decides to force a Bishop-of-opposite-color middlegame.

11.Bxg6	**hxg6**
12.Nb5!	**a6**
13.Nd6 +	**Bxd6**
14.Qxd6	**Na5**

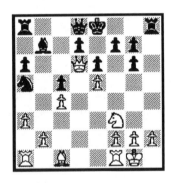

Black appears to have a better Bishop and more solid pawns (15.Nd2 Rc8 and ...Rh4!?-d4) but White has an edge in space.

15.Bg5	**f6**

Of course, not 15...Nxc4 16.Qxc5 Qc8?? 17.Qe7 mate.

16.exf6	**gxf6**
17.Bf4	**Bxf3**
18.gxf3	**g5**

Now 19.Be3 Nxc4 appears to favor Black, as does 19.Bg3 Qe7. White has to work to find counterplay.

19.Bg3	Qe7
20.Qd3	Nc6
21.f4	g4!?

Oversight or sacrifice? Either way it's more promising than 21...Nd4 22.fxg5 f5 23.Be5.

22.Qg6+	Qf7
23.Qxg4	f5

White's Bishop is truly wretched now. If Black has time for ...Nd4 he'll have a powerful position.

24.Qf3	Rb8
25.b4!	

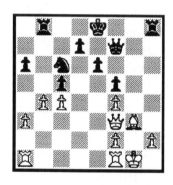

Excellent. White sacrifices a pawn back to point out the advantage he has over Black – the connected White Rooks.

25...	cxb4
26.axb4	Nxb4
27.Rfb1	

Now 27...Qf6, to stop 28.Qc3, would give White a playable game following 28.Ra4.

27...	Nc6
28.Rxb8+	Nxb8

29.Rxa6!

Black may not have seen 29...Nxa6 30.Qa8 +, regaining the Rook.

29...	**0-0**
30.Ra3	**Qg7**

All of a sudden White is a pawn ahead with only the g3-Bishop to serve as compensation. He now prepares to bring it into action via h4 and g5.

31.Qh5	**Nc6**
32.h3	**Qh7!**
33.Qg5 +	**Kf7**
34.Rd3	**Ke8**
35.Qh4	

Clearly, 35.Bh4?? Rg8 will not do, and 35.Kh2 Rh8 36.Bh4 Rg8 is not promising.

35...	**Rh8**
36.Qxh7	**Rxh7**

The endgame is drawn because Black can blockade the c-pawn on the dark square – and because White can protect it on that square against all pressure.

37.Kh2	**Na5**
38.c5	**Kd8**
39.f3	**Kc7**
40.Bf2	**Kc6**
Draw	

6) Robey-Owen, London 1862

1.e4	**b6**
2.d4	**Bb7**
3.Bd3	**e6**
4.Nf3	**c5**
5.c3	**Nf6**
6.Bg5?!	**h6!**

Now White must give up a good Bishop because 7.Bh4 g5 would win a pawn.

7.Bxf6	**Qxf6**
8.Qd2?!	

And this is a further inexact move. White needs the Queen to defend e4. He now loses a pawn.

8...	**Qg6!**
9.0-0	

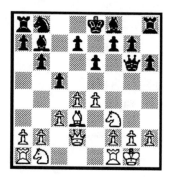

This gambit appears to be White's best bet here.

9...	**Bxe4**
10.Bxe4	

Of course, 10.Ne5?? is not playable, and 10.Nh4 Qh7 goes nowhere.

10...	**Qxe4**
11.Re1	**Qb7**
12.d5	**Be7**
13.c4	

In return for his pawn, White has a nice spatial edge and superior minor pieces (Nc3-e4).

13...	**Bf6**
14.Nc3	**Bxc3?!**
15.Qxc3	**0-0**
16.Rad1	**Qc7**

Black still has problems with his completion of development and might have tried 16...Na6 here.

17.Re4!?	**Qd6**
18.Rg4	

Misguided. With 18.Qc2, threatening 19.dxe4, White retains chances.

18...	**f6**
19.Rg6?	**Nc6!**

This is the trick White missed when he began his flimsy Kingside attack. Now there is little evidence of compensation for White's missing pawn.

20.Qc1	**Ne7**
21.Rg3	**Nf5**
22.Rh3	**Rae8**

If allowed, Black can win by a timely opening of the e-file.

23.g4?	**Ne7**

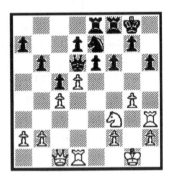

And now the Knight heads powerfully to f4.

24.dxe6	**Qxe6**
25.Rg3	**Ng6**
26.Rd5	**Qe4!**

The threat of 27...Nf4 (and 28...Ne2 + /28...Nxd5) forces White's pieces into even more of a jumble than they already are in.

27.Rf5	**Rf7**
28.b3	**Rfe7**

29.h4	**h5!**
30.Rxf6!?	**hxg4!**

Black won't even be tempted into the complications of 30...gxf6 31.gxh5. The text wins material at no risk.

31.Rd6	**gxf3**
32.Rdxg6	**Qxh4**

The threat of check at e1 decides.

33.Kf1	**Qh1 +**
34.Rg1	**Qh3 +**
35.R6g2	**fxg2 +**

and Black won.

Chapter Four
White Begins with 1.d4

When White begins his game with his d-pawn he creates new positional options that are less frequently seen in 1.e4 b6 games. The struggle for advantage generally turns on whether or not White can secure control of the key light squares at e4 and d5.

On his side, White has the c2-c4 advance and the support of Qc2 or Bd3 to control those two squares. But Black, with ...Bb7, ...Bb4 + and – most of all – ...f7-f5, apppears to have ample ammunition in this battle for crucial vantage points. In this chapter we'll examine more traditional methods by White to fight for the center.

1.d4	**b6**

If Black is interested in the English Defense he may also play 1...e6 and 2...b6 – knowing that he is then tempting White into thinking it will be a French Defense (2.c4 d5).

2.c4

This move can be delayed, so as to take some of the sting out of ...Bb4 +. But if White is trying to gain control of d5 and e4, then Nf3 is not a particularly useful move – and there aren't any other waiting moves that further the strategy of center control.

2...	**e6**

3.Nc3

This is as natural as it is after 1.e4 and 2.d4. However, the problems that arise after 3...Bb4 are considerable and therefore we will consider some rarer alternatives, before attacking more critical 1.d4 lines, in the next chapter.

3...	**Bb4**

Accepting the challenge. Black could, of course, delay this in favor of 3...Bb7, after which 4.e3 or 4.e4 would transpose into lines considered below. The merits of 3...Bb7 include avoiding the 3...Bb4 4.Qb3 line considered later in this chapter. But this is a relatively minor concern.

White now must make a major decision. He can play conservatively, as in a Nimzo-Indian or Queen's Indian Defense, with (a) 4.e3. Or he can take up the gauntlet and go for the massive center with 4.e4, which leads into Chapter Six. He can also prevent the doubling of his c-pawns with the Nimzo-like (b) 4.Qb3 and (c) 4.Qc2.

(a)
4.e3

4.e3

The equally quiet 4.Nf3 turns the opening towards rather stolid but unambitious middlegames for White. For example, 4...Bb7 5.Qc2 f5! 6.a3 Bxc3+ 7.Qxc3 Nf6 with play similar to (c) below, or 5.Qb3 a5 6.a3 Bxc3+ 7.Qxc3 a4 doing a bit of damage to White's Queenside.

4...   Bb7

Again the super-cautious 5.Nf3, transposing into the previous note, presents Black with no troubles and he can obtain a pretty good version of the ancient Dutch Defense lines with 5...f5! 6.Bd3 Nf6 7.0-0 0-0 followed by ...Bxc3, ...d7-d6 and ...c7-c5.

5.Nge2

And 5.a3, as in the comparable Saemisch Variation/Nimzo-Indian position, is questionable because White has difficulty in pushing the e-pawn a la Fritz Saemisch.

We can see that after 5.a3 Bxc3+ 6.bxc3 Nf6 a Nimzo-like position arises that gives White good chances after 7.f3 c5 8.Bd3 Nc6 9.Ne2.

However, 6...f5! is what the English Defense is all about. Then 7.f3 Qh4+ 8.g3 Qh5 9.Bg2 Nf6 10.Nh3 Nc6 11.Nf4 Qf7 and now 12.e4 0-0-0 led to spirited play in Z.Polgar-Rogers, OHRA 1985.

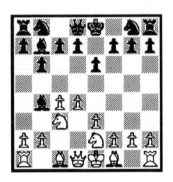

That Knight move is an idea originated by Akiba Rubinstein in the Nimzo-Indian to avert the doubling of the c-pawns. Here 5...Nf6 would, in fact, transpose into a well-known Nimzo position (6.a3 Bxc3+ 7.Nxc3 0-0 8.Bd3 c5 9.d5! with advantage, or 6...Be7 7.d5!).

5...   f5!

Once again this thematic move is needed to discourage White's seizure of e4-control.

6.a3

Consistent with the Rubinstein strategy. Other moves do not justify 5.Ne2 and leave White with developmental problems.

6...   Bd6!?

This strange looking move makes excellent sense in light of Black's Kingside intentions. After 6...Be7 7.d5 Nf6 8.g3! White maintains a firm control of the light squares (8...b5!? 9.Nxb5 exd5 10.Bg2 c6 11.Nbd4 dxc4 12.Qc2 with advantage, as in Eingorn-Rivas, Bor 1986).

7.b4

A recent try at improving over 7.d5 Nf6 8.Nd4 0-0 which was found wanting back in the late 1970's. See Illustrative Game 7.

7...   a5

Black knows when he plays this that he is not stopping White's next move. He simply wants to be better able to exploit the Queenside holes through a later ...axb4.

8.c5   Be7

It appears White is making substantial Queenside progress. But it may come at the cost of prematurely opening the area for exploitation.

9.Rb1

Of course, 9.b5? loses a pawn and 9.cxb6?! is positionally wrong. Perhaps 9.Bb2 is a better try, although 9...Nf6 leaves White with the same problem of how to develop his Kingside without losing the g2-pawn.

9...   axb4
10.axb4   Nf6

11.Nf4

White protects g2 and watches d5 with this move. The ugly-looking 11.f3 may be playable but 11...0-0 12.Ng3 Nc6 leads to a good position for Black (13.Bd3 f4).

11...   0-0

12.Bc4　　　g5!

Black must play energetically to overcome his inferiority in space.

13.Nfe2　　　bxc5

Now 13...Bxg2 14.Rg1 regains the pawn favorably.

14.dxc5

After 14.bxc5 Black fights for the light squares with ...Nc6-a5 and perhaps ...Ne4.

14...　　　Nc6

In this double-edged position White could not prove an edge after 15.f4 gxf4 16.exf4 Qe8 in Plachetka-Kengis, Vienna 1990. A spirited fight emerged after 17.Rf1 Kh8 18.Rf3 Nxb4 19.Rxb4!?. Improvements on White's play are likely, but Black should have just as much room to refine his chances.

(b)
4.Qb3
(after 1.d4 b6 2.c4 e6 3.Nc3 Bb4)
4.Qb3

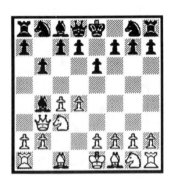

In the comparable Nimzo-Indian position, this is the Rudolph Spielmann idea – attacking the Bishop while preventing the pawn doubling.

4...　　　Nc6!?

This tricky idea, based on 5.a3? Nxd4! (6.Qxb4?? Nc2+), may be suspect for reasons given in the next note. The Queen move can also be handled by 4...c5 or 4...Qe7, e.g. 4...Qe7 5.a3 Bxc3+ 6.Qxc3 Bb7 7.Nf3 d6 followed by ...Nf6-e4/...Nbd7 and ...c7-c5 as in a normal Nimzo-Indian position.

5.Nf3

Too passive to promise any advantage is 5.e3, which can be met by 5...a5 as in the main line. Untested is 5.d5 Nd4 6.Qd1, after which 6...Nf5 7.e4 Ne7 leaves White with a massive center to defend.

5...   a5

The point of this move is not just to provide an answer to the threat of 6.d5, as it may seem.

6.a3   a4!

This time-gainer is a nice way of paralyzing the White Queenside without loss of time.

7.Qc2   Bxc3+
8.Qxc3   Qf6!?

In comparable Nimzo positions (7...Nf6) White obtains a nice game by expanding on the queenside (b2-b4) or pinning the Kingside (Bg5). Here, Black tries to use the absence of ...Nf6 to his advantage.

9.Bg5

After the other natural move, 9.g3, Black could continue 9...Bb7 10.Bg2 Na5 followed by ...Ne7-f5 or ...Nb3.

9...   Qg6

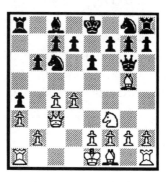

The Black Queen controls an important diagonal from here and also watches the g2-pawn, which may be hanging after the f1-Bishop is developed.

10.e3   Bb7

Black has an excellent game, as illustrated by 11.h4!? f6 12.Bd3 Qf7 13.Bf4 d6 and ...Nge7 (Cooper-Basman, England 1980).

(c)
4.Qc2
(after 1.d4 b6 2.c4 e6 3.Nc3 Bb4)
4.Qc2

Even rarer at the fourth move is 4.Qd3, apparently an idea of Bent Larsen's. After 4...Nf6 5.e4 c5! White's center is under fire.

Larsen himself did not accept the dare of playing 6.d5 exd5 7.cxd5 0-0 (threatening 8...Nxe4 9.Qxe4? Re8) when he faced Jan Timman at Montreal 1979.

That game went 6.dxc5 Bb7! 7.e5 Ne4 8.Ne2 Qh4 and Black more than equalized (9.Be3 Nxc5 10.Qd4 Be4 11.Ng3 Nc6). The alternative of 8.cxb6 Qxb6 9.Be3 Qa5 is another dubious gambit White should avoid.

4...   Bb7

Black continues naturally. Now 5.Nf3 or 5.e3 will reach positions we saw in section (a) earlier in this chapter.

5.a3

The only idea that justifies White's fourth move.

5...   Bxc3 +
6.Qxc3

Now the Nimzo-like 6...Nf6 allows White a freer hand after 7.Bg5 followed by taking control of the light squares.

In fact, the Nimzo proper (1.d4 Nf6 2.c4 e6 3.Nc3 Bb4 4.Qc2) Black almost never plays 4...b6? because it allows 5.e4! with advantage due to center control (5...c5 6.e5 cxd4 7.a3! Bf8 8.Nb5 as in Ree-Andersson, Amsterdam 1979).

6...   f5!

Once more it is this thematic move which gives the opening the English Defense character. Black has enough time to respond to 7.d5 with 7...Nf6 (not 7...exd5 8.Qxg7 Qf6 because of 9.Bh6!).

7.f3

White, who still has his dark-squared Bishop, can afford this kind of loosening move in order to promote control of e4. The more orthodox plans, such as 7.Nf3 Nf6 8.g3 Ne4 or 8.Bg5 h6, allow Black too easy a game.

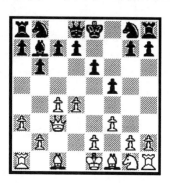

7... Nf6

Note that Black has two good minor pieces trained on e4. After 8.Bg5 Black can probably just expand with 8...h6 9.Bh4 g5!.

8.e3 0-0
9.Qc2

Igor Stohl pointed out that 9.Bd3 allows 9...Ng4! with strong Kingside play, e.g. 10.fxg4 Bxg2 or 10.Ne2 Qh4+ 11.Ng3? Nxh2 or 11.g3 Qh3 12.Nf4 Qh6 13.d5 Nf6 and ...g7-g5.

9... c5!

As soon as White shifts his Queen away from the seemingly-solid d4, Black initiates an attack on that square.

10.Bd3

Now instead of the artificial 10...Nc6? 11.Ne2 Nh5 12.0-0 Qf6 13.b3! and 14.Bb2 (Stohl-Price, Haifa 1989) Black can obtain good chances with 10...cxd4 11.exd4 d5. For example, 14.c5 bxc5 15.dxc5 a5 and ...Ba6.

Illustrative Games

7) Hawkesworth-Plaskett, Hastings 1980-81

1.c4	**b6**

The English Defense is a natural antidote to the English Opening: many players who distrust 1.e4 b6 are unwilling to meet 1.d4 with 1...b6 because White can respond 2.e4. However, after 1.c4 White is locked into a decidedly positional struggle – with or without d2-d4.

2.d4	**e6**
3.Nc3	**Bb4**
4.e3	

Considering the other options available to White, beginning with 4.e4, this timid move is something of a concession that Black has won the battle of the opening.

4...	**Bb7**
5.Nge2	**f5**
6.a3	**Bd6!**

As mentioned earlier, this is the best retreat square.

7.d5	**Nf6**
8.Nd4	**0-0**

White adopts the attractive positional plan of pressuring e6 and closing Black's b7-Bishop out of play.

Note that these two objectives may be mutually exclusive. If White plays dxe6 he allows the b7-Bishop to spring to life. In F.Olafsson-Miles, Las Palmas 1978 White discovered that after 9.dxe6 Black had a strong reply in the form of 9...Ne4!.

White then erred with 10.Qc2 and went downhill rapidly as Black's initiative grew – 10...Nxc3 11.Qxc3 Qf6! 12.exd7 Nxd7 13.Bd2 Nc5 14.Nf3 Qg6.

9.g3   Ne4!

A good move in this position too. Black may follow with a standard blockade strategy of ...Nxc3 and ...e6-e5.

10.Nxe4   fxe4
11.dxe6   Qf6

A gambit comparable to Olafsson-Miles. Now 12.exd7 Nxd7 followed by ...c7-c5 and ...Ne5 looks too hot for White to handle in his undeveloped state.

12.Qe2   Nc6
13.Nxc6

And here 13.exd7 Nxd4 14.exd4 e3 is something best avoided.

13...   Bxc6
14.Bg2   Qxe6

Now with equal material, White has no advantage but rather a deficit in development. And after he fails to play 15.b3, he has the beginnings of a serious disadvantage.

15.0-0?   Ba4!

By a circuitous route, the Bishop is headed for b3 or d3.

16.Bd2   Bc2
17.Qh5   Bd3

A marvelous invasion by the Bishop. Black now doubles Rooks on the f-file because f2 has emerged as the latest weakness.

18.Rfc1   Rf5
19.Qd1   Raf8!
20.Bh3

Black can afford another sacrifice, and this time (20.Be1 Rxf2; 20.f4 exf3!) White must accept.

20...	**Qf7**
21.Bxf5	**Qxf5**

At the cost of the Exchange Black has won virtual control of 32 light squares – particularly of vulnerable ones like f3 and h3.

22.Qe1	**Qh3**
23.Rc3	**Rf5**
24.f4	

If he returns the Exchange with 24.Rxd3 Black inserts 24...Rh5 25.Bc3 before 25...exd3. Then the threat of 26...Qxh2+ is decisive. ·

24...	**exf3**
25.Qf2	**Bxg3!**

White resigns

There will follow 26.hxg3 Rh5 with mate on h1 or h2. Similarly, 26.Qxg3 f2+! and 27...Rg5+ mates.

8) Ibragimov-Kengis, Groningen 1991

1.d4	**e6**
2.c4	**b6**
3.Nc3	**Bb4**
4.e3	**Bb7**

5.Nge2	**f5**
6.a3	**Bd6**
7.d5	**Nf6**
8.g3	

A similar approach to the one seen in the last game but with a difference: White intends to fianchetto both Bishops.

8...	**a5**
9.Bg2	**Na6**

With his last move Black secures c5 for his Knight – at least temporarily. It will be a permanent outpost if White now fails to stop 10...Nc5 and 11...a4.

10.b3!	**Nc5**
11.Bb2	**Qe7**
12.Nd4	**0-0**
13.0-0	

White has carried out the plan of the previous game under better circumstances. He will occupy b5 with a Knight while Black will occupy e4. Chances are very slightly in White's favor.

13...	**Nfe4**
14.Ndb5	

More exact is 14.Qc2!, to undermine the e4-Knight. Then 14...exd5 15.cxd5 Nxc3 16.Bxc3 Ne4 allows White to simply grab the f-pawn.

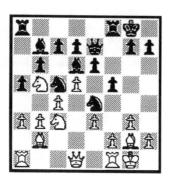

14...	Nxc3!
15.Nxc3	Be5

A nice reorganization by Black. He is preparing to exchange off the Bishop on c3 so as to secure the e4-outpost for his Knight. Then the b2-g7 diagonal looks dangerous but with ...Rf7 Black can turn his attention to the attack on the enemy pawns (e.g. ...d5).

16.Qc2	d6
17.Rfd1	

As usual in such situations, 17.dxe6 is positionally tempting. But 17...Bxg2 and 18...Qxe6, with the idea of 19...a4, eliminates all claim to a White edge.

17...	Bxc3!
18.Bxc3	exd5
19.cxd5	Ne4

Completing the risky-looking strategy. Now a capture on e4 will lead to the same kind of Kingside problems that White had in the previous game.

20.Bb2	Rf7

21.b4?

The point of this move is unclear since Black's c7-pawn is already a backward target. Now Black can open the a-file when he is well prepared for it.

21...	Qe8!
22.Rd4	axb4
23.a4?!	

This may be consistent with his previous move but makes a poor impression. White should have gone into the exchanges with 23.axb4 Rxa1 + 24.Bxa1 Qa8 and then 25.Qd1 Qa2 26.Bxe4! and 27.Rd2. He should not lose the Bishops-of-opposite-color position that results.

23...	**Ra5!**

Preparing to double on the new target at a4, as well as taking aim at the old one at d5. White now makes a disagreeable choice.

24.Bxe4	**fxe4**
25.Rxe4	**Qd7**
26.Rh4	**Qf5**

Material remains equal but it's the pieces that matter: Black has the better Bishop and Rooks. The possible advance of the b-pawn adds a final element that turns the game in Black's favor.

27.e4	**Qf3**
28.Re1	**Rc5**
29.Qd2	**b3**

Else Black would lose the Queen (!) to 30.Re3. Now Black's threat of 30...Rc2 presages a quick conclusion.

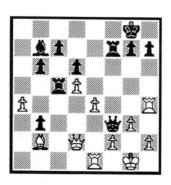

30.Bd4?

But here 30.Rf4 was necessary – and sufficient, because 30...Rxf4 31.gxf4 Rc2 allows White activity with 32.Qd4!.

30...	**Rc2!**

This appears decisive but White has a clever way of prolonging matters.

31.Qg5	Rxf2
32.Qd8 +	Rf8
33.Qxf8 + !	

Trading the Queen for two Rooks and hoping to establish a blockade with his pieces on the dark squares.

33...	Qxf8
34.Bxf2	Qf3
35.Rf4	Qd3
36.Re3	

White's hopes of establishing a fortress with kingside counterchances (Ref3/Bd4) seem remote.

| 36... | b2! |

White resigns

in view of 37.Rxd3 b1 = Q + .

Chapter Five
White Blocks with 3.d5

Ever since the revival of 1...b6 in the 1970's, White has been trying to smash Black's system of development in the most aggressive manner – with a supported d4-d5. Here we consider this primitive – yet dangerous – approach.

1.d4   b6

If White refrains from challenging control of e4 and d5, Black tends to have an easier time of the opening and early middlegame. For example, 2.Nf3 Bb7 3.Bf4 e6 4.e3 is a solid way for White to organize his pieces. But Black should stand well after 4...f5 5.Nbd2 Nf6 6.c3 Be7 7.h3 (to preserve the Bishop against ...Nh5) 7...0-0.

Play could then continue 8.Bd3 Kh8 9.Qc2 d5! (to stop 10.e4) 10.Ne5 c5 11.0-0-0!? Nc6 12.g4 Ne4 with equal chances (Popov-Akopian, Erevan 1977).

2.c4   e6

Now 3.Nf3 Bb7 4.g3 may lead into the Queen's Indian Defense if Black continues 4...Nf6. If Black is looking for an independent line he should avoid the dubious 4...Bxf3 5.exf3 c5 6.d5 exd5 7.Qxd5! with serious problems for Black on the light squares (Spassov-Skrobek, Warsaw 1983). See also Chapter Eight.

3.d5

This is our main concern: White blocks the long diagonal even before Black attempts to occupy it.

3...   Bb7

There has been some dispute over whether this move should be delayed – and the possibility of ...Ba6 is retained. For example, 3...Nf6 is a reasonable try. If White avoids the b4-pin with 4.a3, Black has 4...Ba6!, leaving White with problems to solve.

Nevertheless, we find 3...Bb7 to be more in keeping with Black's overall system. If White had played 3.e4 and then 3...Bb7 4.d5 he would have forced his way into the section that follows regardless of Black's will. The same goes for 3.a3 Bb7 4.d5, which transposes into section (b) below.

(a)
4.e4

4.e4

The most natural way of supporting the d5-pawn is this advance. It has one slight defect – along the e-file – which Black hurries to exploit.

4...   Bb4 +

In this and similar positions, this check was tested often in the 1970's. The general feeling was that if White can avoid 5.Nc3 he should maintain a slight edge. But this is no longer clear.

5.Bd2

On 5.Nc3 we reach a position usually obtained via 3.Nc3 Bb4 4.e4 Bb7 5.d5 and which gives Black excellent chances after 5...Qe7!, threatening 6...exd5.

Meanwhile, the supercautious 5.Nd2 allows Black too free a hand to complete his development satisfactorily. Both 5...Nf6 and 5...Qe7 lead to a good game for Black (5...Qe7 6.Be2 Nf6 7.e5 Ne4 or 7.Qc2 exd5 8.exd5 0-0).

5...   Qe7!

This useful move is also available here. It sets up a major threat of 6...exd5, with pressure down the e-file.

6.Bxb4

On 6.Nc3 exd5 Black can safely grab a pawn (7.Nxd5 Qxe4 + ; 7.cxd5 Nf6). White naturally does not want to mess up his development with 6.Qe2.

6...	**Qxb4 +**

7.Qd2

Even less promising as a gambit is 7.Nd2 Qxb2 or 7.Nc3 Qxb2 8.Nb5 Qb4 + .

7...	**Qxd2 +**

8.Kxd2

Everything seems to be going White's way. He can reinforce his center with 9.Nc3 and enjoy a Queenless middlegame with Bd3 and Nf3-d4. But Black can ensure counterplay if he remains true to the English Defense.

8...	**f5!**

This appears even better than the equalizing 8...Nf6, which led to a quick draw in Timman-Spassky, Hilversum 1983: 9.Nc3 d6 10.Bd3 0-0 11.Nf3 c6! and then 12.dxe6 fxe6 13.e5 dxe5 14.Nxe5 Nbd7 when the isolated e-pawn meant little.

After 8...f5 Black threatens not only to crush the enemy center but to create targets in the White camp (e.g. f2) that White is not ready to defend.

9.f3

On 9.exf5 Black intends 9...exd5!, liberating his b7-Bishop and freeing c6 for his b8-Knight.

9...	**Na6**

We are following Williams-Miles, BBC Master Game 1975. In the televised commentary, Black explained that he didn't know yet where his g8-Knight belonged but there was only one good square for the b8-Knight, so he developed it first.

10.Nc3

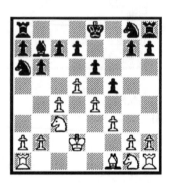

Otherwise the e4-point cannot be maintained.

10...   Ne7

Now the Knight belongs here because of 10...Nf6 11.e5.

11.Bd3   0-0
12.exf5

A major decision. White was concerned in this stem game that 12.Nge2 allows 12...fxe4 13.fxe4 Rf2 strongly.

12...   exd5

The Williams-Miles game now turned in Black's favor after 13.Re1 Nxf5 14.cxd5 Nb4 15.Nh3.

Black now continued 15...Nd6! 16.Be4 a5 17.a3 Na6 after which the d-pawn was encircled (18.Bc2 b5! 19.Ne4 Nc4 +). He eventually won a convincing game.

(b)
4.a3
(after 1.d4 b6 2.c4 e6 3.d5 Bb7)

4.a3

Since 4...Bb4+ proved to be surprisingly uncomfortable after 4.e4, and since 4.Nc3 Bb4 is not so easy to play either, this "Petrosian-like" move has an undeniable appeal. The drawback, of course, is that it is not a developing move: in fact, White has yet to develop a piece. Can Black exploit this?

4...   **Nf6**

Note that under a slightly different move order – 3.a3 Bb7 4.Nc3 – Black may play 4...f5. Then 5.d5 Nf6 leads to play similar to our main line below.

5.Nc3   **Bd6!?**

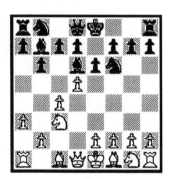

This would seem to be a beginner's error – if you didn't remember that Black was playing ...Bd6 as a retreat in positions considered in the last chapter (3.Nc3 Bb4 4.e3 Bb7 5.Nge2 f5 6.a3 Bd6).

Here, the development of the Bishop on d6 may be no better than on g7 but it may pose greater Kingside problems for White. There is also the possibility of ...Be5!?, as we'll see in the next note.

6.Nf3

On 6.Bg5 Black can get the benefits of a pinning ...Bb4 by way of 6...h6 7.Bh4 Be5!, threatening ...Bxc3+ and ...exd5.Then he should be okay: 8.Qd2 d6 9.Nf3 Bxc3 10.Qxc3 exd5 11.cxd5 Bxd5 (Flear- Forintos, London 1978).

6...   **0-0**

In many Queenside openings Black avoids or delays castling when he has developed his Bishop on c5 or b4 – and White can impose an annoying pin with Bg5.

7.e4

Unpromising is 7.g3 because of 7...Ba6! and there is no convenient way of protecting the c4-pawn, e.g. 8.e3 Qe7! (strong here, too) 9.Be2 exd5 10.cxd5 Ne4 and in Goodman-Miles, Islington 1974 Black was already on top. White did not last long after 11.0-0 Nxc3 12.bxc3 Qe4!.

As noted under the previous move, there is a serious danger here of White imposing a pin. After 7.Bg5 Black may be denied the ...Be5 idea we saw earlier. Perhaps the best reply is 7...h6 8.Bh4 exd5 9.cxd5 (9.Nxd5 g5) Qe7 followed by 10...g5 or 10...c6.

7...   exd5

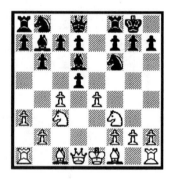

Now 8.cxd5 allows 8...Re8 and if 9.Bg5, then 9...Nxe4! wins material (10.Bxd8 Nxc3 +).

8.exd5   c6

The center is about to collapse. There is no reason to throw in ...Re8 + yet.

9.Be2

Here 9.Bg5 h6 10.Bh4 cxd5 11.cxd5 Na6 and ...Nc7 endangers the d5-pawn.

9...   cxd5
10.cxd5   Na6

11.0-0	**Re8**

Black has a fine position as indicated by 12.Bg5 h6 13.Bh4 Rc8 14.Nd4 Nc5 with equality (Petrosian-Planinc, Moscow 1975).

Illustrative Games

9) Pagden-Patchett, Lloyds Bank 1982

1.c4	**b6**
2.d4	**Bb7**
3.Nc3	**e6**
4.a3	**f5**
5.d5	**Nf6**

Black acknowledges he is willing to play the endgame with a backward e-pawn after 6.dxe6 dxe6.

6.g3	**Bc5**

With a fianchetto on the enemy Kingside Black's Bishop would bite on granite after ...Bd6. But what did Black have in mind against 7.b4 or, a move later, 8.b4?

7.Bg2	**0-0**
8.Nh3	**a5**

That expansion is no longer available. Since we can see Black's b8-Knight going to a6 and his a8-Rook headed for e8, the major unresolved questions of the opening concern White's e-pawn (to e3 or e4 or just remain on e2?) and his c1-Bishop.

9.0-0	**Na6**
10.e4!?	

This thematic attempt to blow apart the enemy light squares may be a bit too ambitious here. For 10.b3 see the following game.

10...	**Ng4!**
11.Nf4	**Qf6**

Black appreciates how much his opponent's 10th move did to weaken the f2-c5 diagonal.

12.exf5   exf5

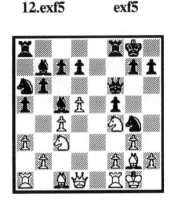

It appears that White's d4-d5 strategy has succeeded in killing the b7-Bishop. But White's c1-Bishop also has some problems that he tries to resolve with his next two moves.

13.Nd3   Rae8

14.Bf4   d6

15.Nb5   Re7

The best thing about Black's game is the e-file. His 14th move acknowledges that he will not try to open matters further with ...c7-c6 and so will live with the pawn structure that currently exists.

16.Nxc5   Nxc5

17.b4

And since 17...Ne4 involves some tactical risk (18.f3) White appears to be gaining the upper hand now.

17...   axb4

18.axb4   Na6

19.Rb1   g5

Otherwise White's initiative on the Queenside becomes too great.

20.Bc1   Ne5

21.f4

Played to avoid 21.Bb2 f4 and ...f3. However, a big hole is now created at e3.

21...	gxf4
22.gxf4	Ng4
23.Nd4	Rg7
24.Ne6?	

Remarkably enough, this is a blunder because it allows the diagonal to be opened.

24...	Qxe6!
25.dxe6	Ne3!

A wonderful combination. Now 26.Qd3 Rxg2 + 27.Kh1 Rg7 + can't be played. White knows he must return the Queen soon.

26.Bxe3	Rxg2 +
27.Kh1	Rg3 + !
28.Qd5	

And this is the way. The trouble is that Black's accurate 27th move costs him a piece.

28...	Bxd5 +
29.cxd5	Rxe3

White resigns

10) Stean-Miles, London 1980

1.c4	b6
2.d4	Bb7
3.Nc3	

One of the disadvantages of 2...Bb7 is that White gets to bring out his b1-Knight with impunity at move three since 3...Bb4 is illegal.

3...	e6
4.a3	f5

White's opening plan is so slow taking shape that this transition to a Dutch Defense makes considerable sense.

5.d5

Otherwise Black may end up with all the benefits of a Dutch without the risk (5.Nf3 Nf6 6.e3?! Be7 7.Bd3 0-0 8.b4 Ne4).

Another good try is 5.f3 Nf6 6.Nh3. Then 6...g6 7.Nf2 Bg7 8.e4 fxe4 9.fxe4 0-0 has been tried successfully (10.Bg5!). But perhaps the Bishop belongs on d6 once again, 6...Bd6 7.Nf2 0-0 8.e4 fxe4 9.fxe4 e5.

5...	Nf6
6.g3	Bc5
7.Bg2	0-0
8.Nh3	

Since the Knight spends the next twenty moves on this square, 8.e3 and 9.Nge2 seems to make more sense.

8...	a5
9.0-0	Na6
10.b3	Qe8

This seems to invite a tactical trick – 11.dxe6 Bxg2 12.exd7. However, Black refutes it with 12...Qe5!, attacking the c3-Knight.

11.Bb2	e5

With this move Black announces he has no intention of trying to dismantle the enemy center at its head (...c7-c6). Instead, he will keep the center relatively closed – and wants the Queenside absolutely sealed. Black's play will emerge on the Kingside.

12.e4	Qg6
13.Qc2	Ng4!

Offering an Exchange sacrifice, since 14.exf5 Qxf5 15.Qxf5 favors White's chances.

14.exf5	Rxf5
15.Be4	Raf8

The sacrifice makes particular sense because of the Knight at h3, which will have only the King to protect it. After 16.Bxf5 Rxf5 17.Qe2 Rh5 18.Kg2 Qf5 Black's threats become overwhelming.

16.Kg2?

This tries to solve the problem of the h3-Knight, with a consolidating f2-f3.

16...	Rxf2 + !
17.Rxf2	Ne3 +

But his 16th move had a tactical hole that temporarily costs him the Queen.

18.Kh1	Nxc2
19.Rxf8 +	Bxf8
20.Bxg6	

There was no choice, of course. But now Black wins the endgame due to weaknesses in the enemy Queenside pawns, specifically b3.

20...	Nxa1

21.Bxh7 +

Or 21.Bf5 Nxb3 and the Knight establishes a stranglehold on the Queenside.

21...	**Kxh7**
22.Bxa1	**Nc5**

Now 23.b4 axb4 24.axb4 Nb3 also costs a pawn. The real problem for White is that after the b3-pawn falls, Black's b7-Bishop suddenly comes to life.

23.Nd1	**Nxb3**
24.Bxe5	**Nd2!**
25.Bxc7	

White is also lost after 25.Ne3 Nxc4! 26.Nxc4 Bxd5 + .

25...	**Nxc4**
26.Nc3	**Bxa3**
27.Ng5 +	**Kg6**
28.Nge4	**b5!**

And the threat of 29...b4 collapses White's remaining hopes.

29.Nxb5	**Bxd5**
30.Nbc3	**Bc6**
31.Kg1	**Bb4**

White resigns

There is little to be done about ...a5-a4-a3-a2.

Chapter Six
White Accepts the 3.e4 Challenge

Undoubtedly the most complex 1.d4 b6 positions arise after White builds his center with 2.c4 and 3.e4. We'll examine them here.

1.d4 b6

A rare idea here is 2.Bg5, intending to mess up Black's pawns with 2...Nf6 3.Bxf6. Black should probably continue 2...Bb7 and then ...d7-d6/...Nd7/...Ngf6 to preserve his pawn structure.

White's Bishop can then end up misplaced. For example, 2.Bg5 Bb7 3.c4 h6!? 4.Bh4 d6 5.Nc3 Nd7 6.e4 Ngf6 7.Bd3 e5 and Black is ready to favorably exchange off the dark-squared Bishop (8.d5 Be7 threatening 9...Nxd5).

In Matera-Soltis, New York 1977 White managed no more than equality after 8.d5 Be7 9.Bxf6! Nxf6 10.Nf3 0-0 11.h4 and 12.g3/13.Bh3.

2.c4 e6

3.e4 Bb7

Now 4.Nc3 is the main line, which we'll consider in the next chapter. Here we'll look at rarer defenses to the e4-pawn, which include (a) 4.f3, (b) 4.Bd3 and (c) 4.Qc2.

(a)
4.f3

4.f3

White is playing the Saemish Variation – but against a different fianchetto. This "Three-and-a-half Pawns Attack" works well against all Black strategies except one.

4...	f5!

Now 5.Nc3 Bb4 transposes into Chapter Seven and other moves run tactical risks (5.Bd3? fxe4 6.Bxe4 Bxe4 7.fxe4 Qh4+ or 6.fxe4 Bxe4 7.Qh5+ g6 8.Qe5 Bxd3 9.Qxh8 Qh4+).

5.exf5

Here the bold of heart will consider the 5...Nh6 gambit. Black appears to be ruining his kingside at the cost of a pawn, but he can meet 6.Bxh6 with 6...Qh4+ and 7...Qxh6.

The most serious test of the gambit was Ree-Miles, Wijk aan Zee 1979, which went 5...Nh6 6.fxe6 Nf5 7.Ne2 Bd6 and now play went off on a strange bend with 8.h4!? 0-0 9.Nbc3 Qf6 10.c5 Be7 11.exd7 Qf7. Eventually a fierce draw was reached.

5...	exf5

The saner approach. Now White's pawn at f3 looks a bit silly (6.Bd3? Qh4+ and 7...Qxd4).

6.Nh3

This maneuver (Nf2) is a good way of making the best out of 4.f3. After 6.Be3 Bb4+ 7.Nc3 Ne7 8.Bd3 0-0 Black may continue ...f5-f4 and ...Nf5-e3.

6... **Bb4+**

Once again this handy tempo-move becomes useful. Now 7.Nd2? hangs a pawn to 7...Qh4+ and 7.Bd2 Qh4+ 8.g3 Qe7+ 9.Kf2 Nf6 turns out rather nicely for Black.

7.Nc3 **Qh4+**

8.g3

After 8.Nf2 Black appears to get sufficient counterplay from 8...Nc6 9.d5 Bc5 or 9...Nd4 10.Be3 Qe7 (11.Qxd4 Bc5).

8... **Qf6**

But here on 8...Qe7+ White should answer 9.Kf2!, after which 9...Bxc3 10.bxc3 Nc6 and 11...0-0-0 is highly double-edged. The text may be more promising, with its pressure on d4.

9.Bg5 **Qf7**

10.Qd3 **Ne7**

The players are headed for castling on opposite wings and a sharp middlegame.

11.0-0-0 **0-0**

Thus far, Vukovic-Schussler, Smederevska Palanka 1979, which led to equal play after 12.Nb5 Na6 13.Bf4 Ng6 and 14...c6.

Since 4.f3 lost much of its point following 5.exf5, attention has focused on other fourth moves in recent years.

(b)
4.Bd3
(after 1.d4 b6 2.c4 e6 3.e4 Bb7)
4.Bd3

Among those alternatives is this natural move. After the less frequently encountered 4.Nd2, Black obtains his usual counterchances with 4...Bb4!, e.g. 5.f3 f5 6.exf5?! Qh4+ 7.g3 Qxd4 or 5.Qc2 Qh4! as in section (c).

At one time the wild 4...f5!? was the center of controversy, with extensive research into 5.exf5! Bxg2 6.Qh5+ g6 7.fxg6 Bg7 8.gxh7+ Kf8 9.Bg5!. Nowadays, 1...b6 defenders prefer a more conservative method.

4...   Bb4+

Unappreciated – or perhaps just under-appreciated – is 4...Nc6, which appears to be a strong alternative in the Owen tradition. After 5.Nf3 Black continues 5...Nb4 and then 6.0-0 Ne7 7.Nc3 Nxd3. See Illustrative Game 11.

5.Bd2

With 5.Nc3 we transpose into the next chapter, while 5.Nd2 reaches the next section, after 5...Qh4 6.Qc2.

5...   **Nc6!?**

The point of this move is that 6.Bxb4 Nxb4 prepares 7...Nxd3 +. Meanwhile, White must defend the d-pawn.

6.Nf3

An indication of this line's antiquity: this position occurred nearly a century and a half ago. In Boden-Owen, London 1858 White played 6.d5 Bxd2 + 7.Qxd2 and after 7...Ne5 8.Nc3 Nh6!? 9.f4 Nxd3 + ?! 10.Qxd3 Black proceeded to self-destruct with 11...f5 12.e5 g5?. Better is 8...Ne7 9.f4 Nxd3 + 10.Qxd3 Ba6 or even 8...Nh6 9.f4 Qh4 +. Black might even try 8...Qh4 + (intending 9...Qg4 or 9...Qh6 10.f4? Qxf4!) but then he must find a good answer to 9.Nb5 (9...0-0-0!?; 9...Qg4).

6...   **Bxd2 +**

7.Nbxd2

Apparently untested is 7.Qxd2, which may prompt Black to try something like 7...Nh6 8.Nc3 Nb4 9.Bb1 f5.

7...   **Qf6**

The lesson for Black is that he must mount an attack on some center pawn. If it isn't the e4-pawn, it must be the d4 one. The text makes sense but perhaps 7...Nh6 and 8...f5 makes more.

8.e5   **Qf4**

This appeared first in Nogueiras-Velez, Cienfuegos 1983 and led to complex play after 9.g3 Qh6 10.0-0 f5! and then 11.d5! Nce7 12.Re1 exd5 13.cxd5 Bxd5 14.Rc1, e.g. 14...Bc6 15.Nd4 or 14...Nc6 15.Bxf5 Nge7 16.Be4 Bf7.

(c)

4.Qc2

(after 1.d4 b6 2.c4 e6 3.e4 Bb7)

4.Qc2

This was Lev Polugayevsky's choice when this recently revived opening was played against him by Viktor Korchnoi in a 1977 candidates match.

4...   Bb4+

A little finesse. On 4...Qh4 White can transpose into our main line with 5.Nd2 Bb4, as that Polugayevsky-Korchnoi game did. But somewhat more promising – once Black has committed his Queen to h4 – is 5.Nc3. Then on 5...Bb4 6.d5 White has better prospects than in our line below.

5.Nd2

With 5.Nc3 we transpose into Chapter Seven. A more placid alternative is 5.Bd2 Bxd2+ 6.Nxd2. Then Kengis' suggestion of 6...Nh6 and 7...f5 deserves a try.

5...   Qh4!

This brings the Queen into action just as White's pieces are vulnerable to harassment. White cannot defend the e4-pawn with 6.f3. So:

6.Bd3   Qg4!?

Raymond Keene's 1977 comment was, "For lovers of risk, 6...Qg4!? could be tried." Apparently there have been few such lovers in master chess because the Queen move had been largely ignored until recently.

This idea doesn't work as well if delayed: 6...f5 7.Nf3 Qg4 8.0-0! and then 8...Bxd2 9.Nxd2 followed by 10.f3.

For a number of years attention has been focused on 6...f5 7.Nf3 Qh5 or 7...Bxd2+ 8.Bxd2 Qg4 without finding a clear path for Black. The text, a favorite of Jaan Ehlvest, appears to strengthen Black's play.

7.Kf1

More or less forced, since 7.Bf1 Bxe4 costs at least a pawn and 7.g3 f5 invites complications not unpleasant for Black.

7...   f5

Of course. The 1...b6 defense is not so difficult to play against 1.d4 when you remember to watch out for three key moves: ...Bb4+, ...Qh4 and the all-important ...f7-f5.

8.f3

Black was not really threatening to gain material by 8...Bxd2 because White could then save his e-pawn with 9.f3. However, 9.a3 Bxd2 10.f3 Qh4 11.Bxd2 fxe4 12.Bxe4 Nc6 must be considered adequate for Black.

8...   Qh4
9.exf5

White might consider 9.Ne2, thinking that on 9...fxe4 he has 10.Nxe4. The problem with this is simple: 10...Qe1 mate! And 10.fxe4 Bxd2 11.Bxd2 Nf6 is going to create problems on the f-file after Black castles.

Better, of course, is 10.Bxe4 after which 10...Bxe4 11.Qxe4 Qxe4 12.Nxe4 Nf6 should be roughly equal.

9...   Qxd4
10.Ne2   Qh4

Half of Black's moves have been with his Queen and he has yet to move a Knight.

This remarkable position first arose in Levitt-Ehlvest, New York 1994 and led to considerable complications after 11.fxe6 Nf6! 12.Ng3 0-0.

Accepting a full pawn with 13.exd7 Nbxd7 followed by ...Ne5 and ...Rae8 appears too risky.

Nevertheless, White seemed to be in trouble after the game continuation – 13.Nde4 Bxe4 (else 14.Bg5!) 14.Bxe4 Nc6 15.exd7 Nh5! since 16.Nxh5 allows that mate on e1 once again.

But after 16.Bd5 + the game was agreed drawn. Short of time, the players were uncertain about the consequences of 16...Kh8 17.Bf4!. Black's chances appear no worse after 17...Nd4.

Illustrative Games

11) Magerramov-Ehlvest, Moscow 1992

1.d4	**e6**
2.c4	**b6**
3.e4	**Bb7**
4.Bd3	**Nc6**

Not only the d4-pawn but also the b4-square is threatened by this Knight move.

5.Nf3	**Nb4**
6.0-0	**Ne7!**

The Knight would probably be misplaced on f6 here. Now it can support ...f7-f5 or go to g6 and concentrate on the Kingside dark squares.

7.Nc3

Threatening to withdraw the Bishop to b1 and thereby forcing Black's hand.

7...	Nxd3
8.Qxd3	Ng6
9.b3	

In Sosonko-Miles, Tunis 1985, White played 9.a3 and a quick draw was agreed upon. Black could have continued with 9...Be7, as in the game, with thoughts of 10...0-0 and 11...f5.

9...	Be7
10.d5	

A natural decision. In the absence of a light-squared Bishop, White wants to compensate with pawn control of those squares.

10...	e5?!

And Black decides to keep matters locked up because he foresees the natural pawn break at its e4 base.

11.Ne2!	0-0
12.Ng3	

Trying to exploit Black's decision at move 10.

12...	d6
13.Nf5	Bc8

White has more space and can force a Bishops-of-opposite-color middlegame anytime he wants. He does not fear ...Bxf5/exf5 because that will leave Black with a bad Bishop. Black must temporize and hope that White overreaches.

14.Bd2	**Re8**
15.Rae1	**Bd7**
16.Kh1	**Bf8**

Good waiting tactics by Black. The onus is now on White to decide how to use his superior heavy pieces: that is, which file to open.

17.g3	**Qc8!**
18.Ne3	**h6**
19.Ng1	**Be7**
20.f4	

This is what Black has been waiting for. His minor pieces now leap into action.

20...	**exf4**
21.gxf4	**Bh4**
22.Re2	**Bf6**
23.Ng2	**b5**

Black's best chance for counterplay (24.cxb5 Qb7 25.a4 a6 26.bxa6 Rxa6 followed by ...Rb8 or ...c7-c6).

24.c5!?	**dxc5**
25.e5	

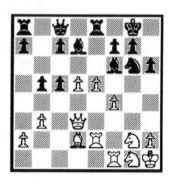

A daring winning attempt that deserved a better fate.

25...	**Bf5**
26.Qxb5	**c6!**

Black must break the central phalanx. Now 27.Qxc5 allows 27...Bd3 and 28.Qxc6 Qxc6 29.dxc6 permits 29...Bd3.

27.dxc6	**Be7**
28.Re3	**Rb8**
29.Qa4	

Trying to hang on to the c6-pawn. After 29.Qe2 Qxc6 White's advantage is not apparent. But he is unaware of the dangers.

29...	**Rb6**
30.c7	**Ra6**
31.Ba5?	

This allows Black to seize the key diagonal.

31...	**Bd7**
32.Qa3	**Bc6!**

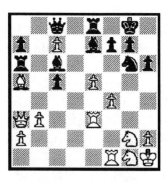

33.Nf3	**Qg4**

Black threatens 34...Nxf4 and provokes a panicked finish by White.

34.e6?!	**fxe6**
35.b4?	**cxb4**
36.Qc1	**Bb7!**
White resigns	

Chapter Seven
Main Line 3.e4 and 4.Nc3

Finally, we reach the crucial main variation of 1.d4 b6 – the main line because it has been analyzed the longest and the most and because it remains the key test of Black's strategy. If White can allow the Nc3/...Bb4 pin and obtain an edge, the whole opening is called into question.

Let's see:

1.d4	b6
2.c4	e6
3.e4	Bb7

Tony Miles has added a new wrinkle to the English defense by playing an early ...Bb4+ before developing the c8-Bishop. We will see ...Bb4+ in a lot of similar positions but Miles' idea is somewhat different and involved ...Nh6 and ...f5, resembling positions we considered in (b) and (c) of the last chapter.

For example, 3...Bb4+ would lead to our main line below after 4.Nc3. The difficult test for Black is to find a good answer to 4.Bd2 Bxd2+ 5.Qxd2!. Miles' solution is 5...Bb7 6.Nc3 Nh6! and then 7.d5 0-0 8.Nf3 f5! 9.Bd3 Na6 10.0-0 Nc5 as in one of his games and 7.Nf3 0-0 8.Bd3 Nc6 9.0-0-0 Ne7 10.d5 d6 as in another.

The crucial line is probably 7.f4 as Anatoly Karpov once used against Miles. Then 7...f5 8.e5 Nf7 9.0-0-0 g5 10.Nf3 Rg8 11.Be2 Na6 was a bit too much of a concession and led to a loss in 35 moves.

4.Nc3

Inviting the pin. Remember that the positions that follow may arise from positions that came up in the last chapter, via 3.e4 Bb7 4.Qc2 Bb4+ 5.Nc3 or 4.Bd3 Bb4+ 5.Nc3.

4...	Bb4

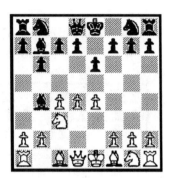

Here we have another wide choice, although we can narrow the field of candidates a bit.

For example, 5.Nge2? was actually played in an international event, Singapore 1979, but is unlikely to be repeated in another – because Black simply wins a pawn with 5...Bxe4.

Also the anti-positional 5.e5? over-extends White's center and allows Black to put too much pressure on d4 after 5...Qh4! and then 6.Nf3 Bxf3 7.Qxf3 Nc6, as in Illustrative Game 12.

The real choice is between (a) 5.f3, (b) 5.Qc2 or (c) 5.Bd3.

(a)
5.f3

5.f3

The other pawn move, 5.d5 allows Black to add immediate pressure on the center with 5...Qe7!, as we saw in similar situations in Chapter Five.

For example, 6.Be2 Nf6 7.f3 exd5 8.cxd5 c6 and Black stood excellently in Polgar-Speelman, 1993 (9.dxc6 Nxc6 10.Nh3 d5! 11.exd5 0-0-0 with a ferocious attack that won in seven more moves).

5...   f5

The same response we saw with the moves Nc3 and ...Bb4 omitted.

6.exf5

Here 6.e5 would play into Black's positional plan. He would then try to encircle the d4/e5 pawn chain with ...Nh6-f7/...Nc6. For example, 6...Nh6 7.a3 (not

7.Bxh6? Qh4+ and 8...Qxh6) 7...Bxc3+ 8.bxc3 Nc6 9.Nh3 Nf7 10.Bd3 Qh4+ 11.Nf2 Qe7 and 12...Na5 as in Kraidman-Keene, Natanya 1977.

6...   **Nh6!?**

The Knight is headed for f5, where it will add strength to ...Qh4+. Now 7.Bd3 Qh4+ 8.g3 Qxd4 or 8.Kf1 Bxc3 and 9...Nxf5 should be fine for Black. See Illustrative Game 13.

7.fxe6   **Nf5**

Now the full gambit line of 8.exd7+ Nxd7 offers Black rapid development and pretty good compensation because of the threats to the d4-pawn and of ...Qh4+.

For example, 9.Bf4 0-0 10.Qd2 c5 11.dxc5 Qe7+ and now 12.Qe2 Bxc3+ 13.bxc3 Qf6 led to problems for White in Plaskett-Drury, Smethwick 1983.

8.Bf4

Too risky is 8.Bd3 because of 8...Qh4+ 9.Kf1 0-0! (better than 9...Ng3+ 10.hxg3 Qxh1 11.exd7+ with good compensation for the Exchange).

There may follow 10.Bxf5 Rxf5 11.Be3 dxe6 12.Bf2 Qf6 13.Nge2 (Ilincic-Litus, Yugoslavia 1933) and now 13...Nd7! 14.Ng3 Rxf3 is recommended in the *Informant*.

8...   **dxe6**

This is the conservative alternative to 8...Qh4+ 9.g3 Qe7, which may also be adequate.

9.Qa4+   **Nc6**

10.d5

Queenside castling worked out okay here for White in Conquest-Plaskett, Hastings 1987-88 following 10.0-0-0 Nxd4 11.Nh3 0-0 12.Kb1.

This is better than 11.Be5 Bc5!, which is based on 12.Bxg7? Qg5+ and 12.b4 0-0!.

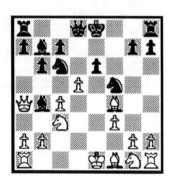

10...   Bxc3+!

An improvement on 10...exd5 11.0-0-0 Bxc3, which can be answered strongly by 12.cxd5. Then if 12...Qf6 then 13.dxc6 Bxb2+ 14.Kb1 and White stood better in Lev-Kengis, Lloyds Bank 1991.

11.bxc3	**exd5**
12.cxd5	**Qxd5**

Now according to the *Informant*, White has compensation after 13.Bc4 Qc5! 14.0-0-0 – yet 14...Nd6 remains to be tested. Altogether, 10...Bxc3+ seems to strengthen Black's resources sufficiently. We can now turn our attention to the second defense of the threatened e-pawn, 5.Qc2.

(b)
5.Qc2
(after 1.d4 b6 2.c4 e6 3.e4 Bb7 4.Nc3 Bb4)
5.Qc2

The Queen move seems to make more sense here than with Nc3 and ...Bb4 omitted. But again Black's Queen can create chances with a Kingside incursion.

5...   Qh4

This move may have originated with Sonya Graf, the German-American master whose use of it we witnessed in the Introduction. When Miles revived it in the late 1970's, his countryman William Hartston remarked in the "British Chess Magazine" that he recalled seeing it mentioned somewhere before "in analysis (if only a joke)."

It's more than a joke. Now, for example, 6.d5 is met nicely by 6...f5, e.g. 7.exf5 exd5!, and now 8.Nf3 Qe4+ 9.Qxe4 dxe4 is a favorable endgame for Black.

6.Bd3   f5

This based, of course, on 7.exf5? Bxg2.

7.Nf3

More accurate than 7.g3 Bxc3+ 8.bxc3 Qh5 with holes in the Kingside to exploit, e.g. 9.f3 fxe4 10.fxe4 Nf6 11.Ne2 Qf3 12.Rf1 Qg2 (Kharlov- Brodsky 1991), or simply 7...Qh5 8.Be2 Qf7 9.f3 fxe4 10.fxe4 Nf6 11 d5 0-0 (Farago-Miles, Hastings 1976-77).

7...   Qg4

The Queen stood well on this square in comparable 4.Qc2 positions. White tries to find a difference.

8.0-0   Bxc3
9.h3!

Here's one important difference: the Queen is pushed away from squares that pressure e4.

9...   Qh5
10.bxc3

Now 10.Qxc3 fxe4 11.d5 Nf6 and White loses material.

10...   Nf6

Black's pressure on e4 is maximized now and 11.exf5 Bxf3 doesn't look too promising.

11.Nd2

This position was known nearly twenty years ago and considered roughly equal. Remarkably, there has been very little testing of it since then. Play may continue 11...fxe4 12.Nxe4 Nc6 13.Bf4 0-0-0!? but 11...Qg6 12.d5 looks too risky.

(c)
5.Bd3
(after 1.d4 b6 2.c4 e6 3.e4 Bb7 4.Nc3 Bb4)
5.Bd3

This leads to the most interesting complications because Black's best response is:

5...   f5

In contrast with 4.Bd3 f5 positions, this thrust has a better reputation here, especially since f8 is available for Black's King in the crucial 6.exf5 line.

(see diagram next page)

6.Qh5 +

This odd move has ended up as the main line if only because no others have performed any better, and several have not done as well at all.

For example:

(a) 6.exf5? Bxg2 7.Qh5 + Kf8 and White's compensation is not visible.

(b) 6.d5 fxe4 7.Bxe4 Qh4! and White's center is crumbling, e.g. 8.Qe2 Nf6 9.Bf3 0-0 10.dxe6 Nc6! 11.Be3 Ne4 with excellent play for Black (Kaplan-Miles, Sao Paulo 1977). See also Illustrative Game 14.

(c) 6.Qc2 and now 6...Nc6 may be the way to respond, e.g. 7.Nf3 fxe4 8.Bxe4 Nf6 (9.d5? Nxe4 10.dxc6 Bxc6; 9.Bg5 Be7).

6...   g6
7.Qe2

Now we can see that the check at h5 is better than the immediate 6.Qe2 which allows Black an easy game after 6...Nf6. Then White has nothing better than 7.Bg5! fxe4 8.Bxe4 Bxc3 + 9.bxc3 Bxe4 10.Bxf6 Qxf6 11.Qxe4 Nc6.

7...   Nf6

Now 8.e5? is simply an error: 8...Bxg2 9.exf6 Qxf6! 10.Bf4 Nc6 and White has insufficient compensation for the loss of the Exchange.

8.Bg5

This appears better than 8.f3 which allows 8...Nc6 (which is superior to the trick 8...fxe4 9.fxe4 Nxe4 10.Bxe4 Bxc3 + since then not 11.bxc3 Qh4 + but 11.Kd1! gives White the advantage). After 8...Nc6 White should play 9.Be3 f4 10.Bxf4 with mixed chances. See Illustrative Game 15.

8...   fxe4

9.Bxe4

Perhaps 8.Bc2 is more accurate: 9...c5?! 10.d5! exd5 and now 11.0-0-0 led to chances for both sides in Shirazi-Bordonada, Tiruch Irapalli 1978. Black might try something like 9...Be7.

Black also can, however, play a little less sharply with 9...Qe7. Then on 10.0-0-0 he has 10...Bxc3 11.bxc3 Nc6 with a fine game (O. Rodriguez-Keene, Alicante 1977), e.g. 12.f3 e3 13.Qxe3 Na5 14.Qe5 Qa3+ 15.Kb1 Nxc4.

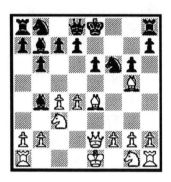

9...	Nxe4!

Black gets a pretty good game with 9...Nc6 but the text gives Black excellent tactical chances.

10.Bxd8	Nxc3

11.bxc3

On 11.Qe5 0-0 12.bxc3 Bxc3+ 13.Kf1 Bxa1 White can try to raid the Queenside with 14.Qxc7 Nc6 15.Qxb7. This occurred in Robey-Regan, New York 1975 and led to balanced chances after 15...Raxd8.

11...	Bxc3+
12.Kf1	Bxa1
13.Bxc7	Bxd4

Black has a Rook, Bishop and a pawn for the Queen – a pretty good form of compensation. In terms of positional compensation, he has two excellent Bishops and a King that will likely be more secure for some time. He can also plant a Knight effectively on d4 after his Bishop shifts to g7 or c5.

See Illustrative Game 16 for an example of the Queen sacrifice succeeding.

Illustrative Games

12) Murey-Garcia, Moscow 1982

1.c4	e6
2.Nc3	b6
3.d4	Bb4
4.e4	Bb7
5.e5?!	

As mentioned earlier, if White is going to push one of his center pawns, 5.d5 makes more sense. Then 5...Qe7! looks best, setting up a threat along the e-file of ...exd5.

For example, 6.Be2 Nf6 7.Qd4 exd5 8.exd5 Qe4! turned out excellently in Tartakover-Reti, Goteborg 1920. It's better for White to block the e-file with 6.Be3 so that he can bring out his other Bishop to d3. But 6.Be3 exd5 7.exd5 Nf6 8.Bd3 c6 was fine for Black in Haik-Benjamin, London 1978.

5...	Qh4
6.Nf3	Bxf3!?

A surprising but quite justified decision. Now d4 comes under heavier fire.

7.Qxf3	Nc6
8.Bf4!	Rc8

Unpinning the c6-Knight and threatening the d4-pawn.

9.g3	Qe7

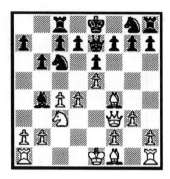

Black's Queen is preparing to roam the queenside now, e.g. 10...Bxc3 + 11.bxc3 Qa3.

10.0-0-0	**Bxc3**
11.Qxc3	**Qb4**
12.Qc2	**Qa5**
13.d5?	

Too much too fast. White's two Bishops offer him excellent prospects if he takes the proper precautions. Better was 13.a3.

13...	**exd5**
14.cxd5	**Nb4**
15.Qc4!	**Ne7**

Now 15...Nxa2 + 16.Kb1 was too risky for a player with only one Knight and his Queen in play.

16.Bd2	**c5**
17.a3	**Qa4**

And here 18.axb4 cxb4 + justifies the earlier ...Rc8. But the pinned Knight can't run away.

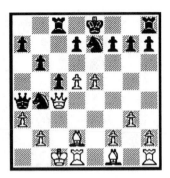

18.Bg2	**b5!**
19.Qe4	**Qb3!**
20.axb4	**cxb4 +**

White finally must accept the sacrifice but may not have realized how strong it was.

21.Kb1	**Rc4**
22.Be3	

After 23.Qe2 Black wins with 23...Qc2 + and 24....b3!, setting up the mating check at a4.

22...	**Rxe4**
23.Bxe4	**0-0**

At last Black gets to castle. The White Bishops remain impressive but Black should be able to consolidate fairly easily once his Queen returns to play.

24.Rd4	**Rc8**
25.Rc1	**Rxc1 +**
26.Bxc1	**g6**

First step, secure King safety. Next: get the Queen off b3 and into the real world.

27.Be3	**Qa4**
28.g4	**Kg7**

White makes his bid for counterplay now.

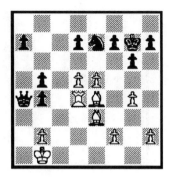

29.e6!?	**dxe6**
30.dxe6	**fxe6**
31.Bc2	**Qa5**
32.Rd7	**b3!**

Just in time. The position was beginning to become critical (32...Kf6 33.Bb3 and Bc5).

33.Bxb3	**Qe1 +**
34.Bd1	**Kf6!**
35.g5 +	**Kf5**
36.Kc1	**Nd5**

All of a sudden the King is safe at f5 and Black's Knight joins a surprising attack. The rest of the game is marred by time trouble.

37.Bd2	**Qf1**
38.Rxa7	**Ke5**
39.Rxh7	**Qc4 +**
40.Bc2	**Qf1 +**
41.Bd1	**Qxf2**

(see diagram next page)

To win Black needs a passed pawn or a mate.

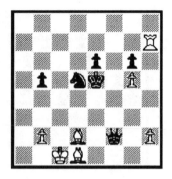

42.h4	Qc5 +
43.Kb1	Qd4
44.Kc1	Qc4 +
45.Bc2	Qf1 +
46.Bd1	b4
47.Rb7	Qa6

Now if the Rook leaves the b-file, Black wins with 48...Qa1 + 49.Kc2 b3 + .

48.Rb8	Qa7!

White resigns

13) Drilinsh-Kengis, Latvian Ch. 1990

1.d4	e6
2.c4	b6
3.Nc3	Bb7
4.e4	Bb4
5.f3	f5
6.exf5	Nh6
7.Bd3?!	

For better or worse, this is one gambit best accepted. Now Black gets the same amount of active play at no material risk.

7...	Qh4 +

8.Kf1

As noted earlier, 8.g3 Qxd4 is no improvement.

8...	**Bxc3**
9.bxc3	**Nxf5**
10.Nh3	

Allowing 10...Ng3 + would be too risky here. This move allows the Bishop to be developed on g5 with tempo.

10...	**0-0**
11.Bg5	**Qh5**
12.Kg1	**Nc6**

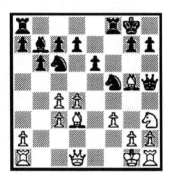

Black has a variety of plans, including the attack on g2 with ...Nh4 and on c4 with ...Na5. He would also like to open the center with a timely ...e6-e5xd4. The tactical idea of 13...h6, clearing h4 in preparation for ...Nh4xg2, is strongest.

13.Qd2	**h6**
14.Bf4	**Nh4!**
15.Nf2?	

Completely unsuspecting. Better was 15.Rf1.

15...	**Nxg2!**
16.Kxg2	**Nxd4!**

The triple attack on f3 is decisive. Now 17.cxd4 Qxf3 + 18.Kf1 Rxf4 is deadly.

17.Qe3	**Nf5!**

Better than an immediate capture on f3 since 18.Qe2 allows ...Bxf3 + 19.Qxf3 Nh4 + .

18.Bxf5	**Rxf5**

The doubling of Rooks on the f-file proves decisive.

19.Ne4	**Raf8**
20.Bg3	**Rxf3**
21.Qd4	

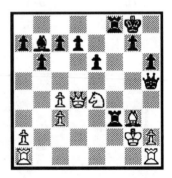

21...	**Rxg3 + !**
22.hxg3	**Qf3 +**

White resigns

Not waiting for 23.Kh3 Bxe4 and 24...Qh5 mate.

14) Whiteley-Keene, Cambridge 1976

1.e4	**e6**
2.d4	**b6**

Yes, this is also a valid method of reaching the English Defense.

3.c4	**Bb7**
4.Bd3	**Bb4 +**
5.Nc3	**f5**
6.d5?!	

As noted earlier, this attempt to close the b7-Bishop's diagonal is too little too late.

6...	**fxe4**
7.Bxe4	**Qh4!**
8.Qd3	

Black now gains a lead in development by harassing the enemy King, Queen and d5-pawn.

8...	**exd5**
9.cxd5	**Nf6**
10.Bf3	**Ba6**
11.Qe3 +	**Kf7**

With the clear threat of 12...Re8.

12.Qf4	**Re8 +**
13.Kd1	**Qxf4**

Black might like to stay in the middlegame but has no choice now.

14.Bxf4	**Bxc3**
15.bxc3	**d6**

Black intends to surround the d5-pawn with ...Bc4 while dominating the e-file with Rooks.

16.Nh3	**h6**
17.Kc2	**Bc4!**

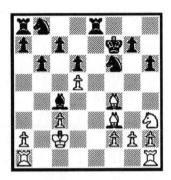

18.Rhd1	**Nbd7**
19.a4	

Expressing concern about ...b6-b5 and ...Nb6xd5.

19...	**Nc5**
20.Rd4	**Be2!**
21.Bxe2	

Bringing the Knight into play with 21.Ng1 Bxf3 22.Nxf3 costs a pawn after 22...Re2+

21...	**Rxe2+**
22.Kd1	**Rae8**

White has avoided losing material but is just hanging on. Now 23...Re1+ is threatened.

23.Ra3	**Re1+**
24.Kc2	**R8e2+**
25.Bd2	**Rh1**
26.c4	**Rxh2**
27.a5	

White's best chance is the creation of a Queenside target. Now 27...Rxg2 walks into the fork on f4.

27...	**Re7**
28.axb6	**axb6**
29.g4	**Re4**

30.Rxe4	**Ncxe4**
31.Rf3	**g5**

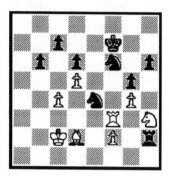

Black fixes the pawn at g4 and prepares to win it after ...Kg6.

32.Be3	**Kg6**
33.Kd3	**Nc5 +**
34.Bxc5	

Not much choice here (34.Ke2 Nxg4).

34...	**bxc5**
35.Rg3	**Nxg4!**

Winning a second and ultimately decisive pawn (36.Rxg4 Rxh3 +).

36.Ke2	**Kh5**
37.Ke1	**Ne5**
38.Kf1	**Kh4!**
39.Ng1	**g4**
40.Rc3	**Kg5**
White resigns	

15) Adorjan-Spassky, Taluca 1982
Rarely has a Candidates-match player suffered a defeat in an Interzonal as badly as White does in this.

1.c4	**b6**

2.d4	Bb7
3.Nc3	e6
4.e4	Bb4
5.Bd3	f5
6.Qh5 +	g6
7.Qe2	Nf6
8.f3	Nc6!

White's last move is actually an offer of a good gambit: 8...fxe4 9.fxe4 Bxc3 + 10.bxc3 Nxe4 11.Nf3! (not 11.Bxe4 Qh4 +).

9.e5?

Much better was 9.Be3 f4 and now not 10.Bf2 e5 11.a3 Nxd4 but simply 10.Bxf4 Nxd4 11.Qf2. Black stands well then with 11...Nc6. And if 12.0-0-0, then 12...Bxc3 and 13...Qe7.

9...   Nxd4!

White must have assumed this was not playable because of...

10.Qf2   Nh5

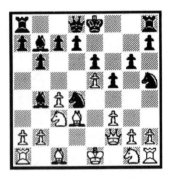

Only now did White notice 11.Qxd4 Bc5. But since 11.g4 fxg4 12.Qxd4 allows 12...Qh4 + with a probably decisive attack, he decided to throw himself on Black's sword.

11.Qxd4   Bc5
12.Qxc5

Sadly, there was nothing better now.

12...	**bxc5**
13.Be3	**Qh4 +**
14.g3	**Nxg3**
15.Bf2	**f4!**

This saves the pinned Knight and preserves his huge material edge.

16.Be4	**0-0-0**
17.0-0-0	**Ne2 +**
18.Ngxe2	**Qxf2**

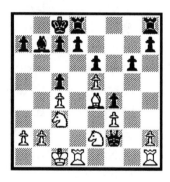

White can resign. Black will decide the game by opening the d-file.

19.Rhf1	**Qe3 +**
20.Rd2	**d5**
21.Nd1	**Qxd2 +!**

Fastest: a Queen-versus-two-Knight middlegame is turned into an Exchange and two pawns down ending.

22.Kxd2	**dxe4 +**
23.Kc2	**g5**
White resigns	

16) Gouret-Prie, Paris 1990

1.c4	**b6**

2.Nc3	e6
3.e4	Bb7
4.d4	

Or 4.Nf3, transposing into our final chapter. As we'll see there, White runs considerable positional risk of turning d4 over to Black as an outpost.

4...	Bb4
5.Bd3	f5
6.Qh5+	g6
7.Qe2	Nf6
8.Bg5	fxe4
9.Bxe4	Nxe4!

A sound sacrifice and not very difficult to evaluate.

10.Bxd8	Nxc3
11.bxc3	Bxc3+
12.Kf1	Bxa1
13.Bxc7	Bxd4
14.Nf3	Bc5

Now 15.Be5 and 16.h4 looks best.

15.Qe5?	0-0

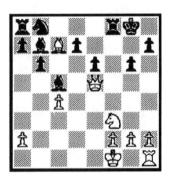

The White Queen only blocks the c7-Bishop. White probably counted on 16.Bd6 but 16...Nc6 17.Qg3 Rf5 doesn't solve his undeveloped Kingside. So...

16.Bxb8?!	**Raxb8**
17.h4	**Rbc8**
18.h5	**Rf5**

After this Black is clearly in the driver's seat.

19.Qc3	**Bxf3**

The alternative of 19...g5 does improve after 20.Rh3 g4 21.Rg3.

20.gxf3	**g5!**
21.Qd3	**Rc7**
22.Rg1	**Be7**
23.Rg4	**Kf7**

Since White can no longer change the pawn structure (except by sacrificing the f3-pawn) Black begins to maneuver his pieces around in search of a winning formation.

24.Rd4	**Ke8**
25.Rg4	**h6**
26.Kg2	**Bf6**
27.Re4	**Ke7**

Note that White can't even force a trade of Rooks because Black controls all the likely squares for that exchange.

28.Kg3	**Be5 +**
29.Kg2	**d6!**
30.Re2	**Kf7**

Black finds his plan: his King belongs at g7 and his Rooks at f7 and f5.

31.Re4	**Kg7**
32.Re3	**Rcf7**
33.Qe4	**g4!**

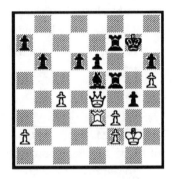

Decisive (34.Qxg4 Rg5; 34.fxg4 Rxf2+ 35.Kh3 Rh2 mate).

34.f4	**Bxf4**
35.Qxe6!?	**Bxe3**
36.fxe3	**Rxh5**
37.Qxd6	**Rg5!**

With no prospects of perpetual check, White has no defense to the advance of the g-pawn.

38.e4	**g3**
39.e5	**Rf2+**
40.Kg1	**g2**
White resigns	

Chapter Eight
White Avoids d2-d4

In this chapter we'll consider the closed-center positions that arise when White treats the opening like a King's Indian Reversed, a Reti or English Opening, or some other hypermodern offshoot.

Black's strategy should not change much: he still looks for ...Bb4xc3 and the pressuring of e4. There is less incentive to bring his Queen out because the position takes on a more positional character.

(a)
The English Opening versus English Defense I
1.c4   b6

Now White will avoid 2.d4, transposing into the four previous chapters, and concentrate instead on a traditional English Opening development (Nf3/Bg2).

2.Nc3

Note that on 2.Nf3 Bb7 3.g3 Black can try to cripple the enemy pawn structure with 3...Bxf3!? 4.exf3 c5. If White allows 5...Nc6 and latter ...Nd4, Black should be at least equal, as has been shown in similar positions of the English Opening with colors reversed (1.c4 c5 2.b3 Nf6 3.Bb2 g6 4.Bxf6!? exf6 5.Nc3).

But there is a difference between that English position and the 1.c4 b6 2.Nf3 Bb7 3.g3 Bxf3 4.exf3 c5 one. White can fight for control of d4 with 5.d4!, after which Black's best is probably 5...Nc6! 6.d5 Nd4 7.Be3 e5 with unclear play.

3...   Bb7
3.Nf3   e6

A White e4 (instead of the following g3) is a more important test of Black's play and will be considered in section (b).

4.g3

Here 4.e3 is a quiet treatment of the opening but not without bite. After 4...Nf6 5.b3 c5 6.Bb2 Be7 we are headed into an English Opening in which the c- and d-pawns will be traded off fairly early (e.g. 7.Be2 0-0 8.0-0 d5 9.cxd5 exd5 10.d4 Nbd7 11.Rc1 Rc8 12.Rc2 a6 13.dxc5 bxc5 – Andersson-Planning, Benja Luka 1976).

| **4...** | **Bb4** |

The addition of Nc3 and ...e6 make the 4...Bxf3 5.exf3 c5 strategy less appealing because of 6.d4 Nc6 7.d5 Nd4 8.Be3 and now 8...e5 would cost Black a tempo compared with the earlier line. This may not matter in a semi-closed position.

Black should, however, avoid 8...Nf5 9.Bh3 Ngh6 because of 10.Qa4! g6 11.0-0 with a strong game (11...Nxe3 12.fxe3 exd5 13.Rad1! – Davies-Plaskett, England 1991).

5.Bg2

Preventing the doubling of the pawns is desirable but 5.Qc2 makes 5...Bxf3 attractive again (6.exf3 Nc6 and ...Nd4).

| **5...** | **Bxc3** |

6.bxc3

Now on 6.dxc3, with the idea of Qc2 and e2-e4, Black can control that square with 6...Nf6 followed by moving his center pawns one square, to d6 and e5. Then with ...a7-a5 and ...Nbd7-c5 he can establish strong minor piece play.

| **6...** | **Ne7** |

Here the Knight seems more appropriate on e7, since White can control e4 with a pawn (6...Nf6 7.d3 0-0 8.0-0 d6 9.e4).

7.0-0   0-0

8.a4

This doesn't look right because it weakens the b3 square, which Black eyes with his Knight in two moves. No better is 8.d4, which leaves the c4-pawn without adequate support after 8...d6 and ...Nb8-c6-a5.

The better try is 8.d3, and if 8...c5, then 9.a4 Nbc6 10.Nd2, intending 11.Nb3. After 10...Na5 Black appears to stand quite well. Also, on 9.e4 (instead of 9.a4) Black should continue 9...Nbc6, and if 10.Nh4, then 10...d5.

8...   Nbc6

9.d3   Na5!

Black prepares an attack on the Queenside mixed with ...f7-f5. In Pigusov-Ehlvest, Novosibirsk 1993 he obtained excellent play following 10.e4 f5 11.exf5 Nxf5. See Illustrative Game 17.

(b)
Second Round: English versus English

Another English strategy calls for White to put his e-pawn on the fourth rank before deciding what to do with his f1-Bishop. We'll consider this idea next.

1.c4

If Black is going to play 1...b6, probably the least useful of the many reasonable opening moves for White is 1.Nc3. The reason is that White cannot get into a normal 1.d4 English Defense because he has blocked his c-pawn. And if he plays into 1.e4 lines he will have to consider the possibility of ...Bb4, as we saw in Chapter One.

Also, since Nc3 blocks the c-pawn, Black can consider more extravagant strategies on the light-squares, such as ...Bxf3. See Illustrative Game 19.

1...	b6
2.Nc3	e6
3.e4	

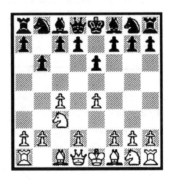

Since the recurring theme of the English is the control of d5, this move is fully in alignment with White's intentions. But now White will not, however, be able to fianchetto his Bishop on g2 smoothly.

3...	Bb7
4.Nf3	

Viktor Korchnoi has tried 4.Nge2 here to avoid the doubling of his pawns after ...Bxc3. The problem with this is 4...Nf6!, since 5.e5 Ng8 and 6...d6 will exploit the misplacement of White's e2-Knight and over-extended center.

4...	Bb4
5.Qb3!?	

Better than 5.Bd3 Ne7 preparing ...f7-f5. For example, 6.0-0 0-0 followed by 7...f5, e.g. 7.Ne2? f5! 8.Qc2 Na6! and White is in trouble. See Illustrative Game 20.White can do better than 7.Ne2. For example, 7.Re1 f5 and now 8.e5? runs into trouble after 8...Ng6 9.Bf1 Bxf3! (see Illustrative Game 21). But 8.a3! liquidates the danger and leads to level play.

5...   **Na6**

The tempting 5...Bxc3 6.Qxc3 Bxe4 turns out poorly after 7.d3 Bxf3 and now 8.Qxg7 Qf6 9.Bh6! as in Knott-K.Arkell, British Championship 1985.

After 9...Qxg7 10.Bxg7 Black gets a pawn for the Exchange but White retains the better chances in the endgame.

6.d3

Note that 6.a3 now fails to 6...Nc5!. Then 7.Qxb4 a5 allows the Queen to be trapped. And on 7.Qc2 Black wins a pawn with 7...Bxc3 8.Qxc3 Bxe4! because the previous trick – 9.d3 Bxf3 10.Qxg7 Qf6 11.Bh6 – fails here to 11...Qxh6! 12.Qxh8 Nb3! with a killing attack.

6...   **Ne7**

Black develops similar to the way he did in section (a). White's f1-Bishop doesn't have much of a future in this closed position. A likely continuation would be 7.a3 Nc5! 8.Qc2 (again 8.Qxb4 a5 is a trap) 8...Bxc3 + 9.Qxc3 a5.

(c)
The King's Indian Reversed versus the English Defense

The K.I.R. is characterized by the moves Nf3, g2-g3, Bg2, d2-d3 and e2-e4. Time and ample experience has shown it can be used against just about any Black formation of pawns and pieces. The question is: does it gain an edge against 1...b6?

1.Nf3   **b6**

Now if 2.e4 Bb7 3.Nc3 e6 4.d4 Bb4 we transpose into Chapter One. And 2.e4 Bb7 3.d3, as we saw, allows Black a good 3...d5!.

2.g3   **Bb7**

3.Bg2

3...   **c5**

Playing the position like an old style Dutch Defense carries with it certain positional risks on the light squares. For example, 3...f5 4.0-0 Nf6 5.d4 a6 6.c4 Be7 invites a dangerous 7.d5! exd5 8.Nd4 or 8.Nh4.

4.d3

White's pawn structure in the center will consist of d2-d3 and e2-e4.

4...   **g6**

Black can also play 4...d5 5.0-0 Nf6 6.Nbd2 e6 although this does not stop White from playing 7.e4 dxe4 8.Ng5.

5.0-0   **Bg7**

6.e4

White can also treat the position like an English with 6.c4, after which ...Nf6 and ...d7-d5 is a natural way of handling Black. The text, with its promise of f2-f4-f5, is sharper.

6...	Nc6
7.Nbd2	**Nh6**

Black retains the option of attacking the center with ...f7-f5.

8.Nh4	**0-0**
9.f4	

9...	f5

Black should not allow 10.f5!.

10.e5	**Qc7**

A somewhat unusual delay by Black in advancing either the d- or e-pawn. If allowed a free hand, White will make his advantage in space felt. Black, however, can pressure the enemy center with ...d7-d6 or ...g7-g5.

For a good example of his resources, see Illustrative Game 18.

Illustrative Games

17) Pigusov-Ehlvest, Novosibirsk, 1993

1.Nf3	**b6**
2.c4	

It is White's difficulty in controlling e4 now that makes Black's system so attractive against 1.Nf3.

2...	**Bb7**
3.Nc3	**e6**
4.g3	**Bb4**
5.Bg2	**Bxc3**

In the 1970's anti-English Opening systems with ...Bb4xc3 became popular after it was discovered how difficult it can be for White to change his fixed pawn structure.

6.bxc3	**Ne7**
7.0-0	**0-0**
8.a4	**Nbc6**
9.d3	**Na5**
10.e4	

White needs some positional compensation for his doubled pawns and the two Bishops are not enough. Now 10...d5 comes into question but Black has another idea.

10...	**f5**
11.exf5	

After 11.e5 Ng6 White ends up with two doubled pawns and no clear method of opening the position for his heavy pieces.

11...	**Nxf5**
12.Bf4	**Ne7!?**

The Knight will be redeveloped on g6.

13.Be3	**Ng6**
14.Ng5	**Bxg2**
15.Qh5?!	

The normal recapture 15.Kxg2 was superior. White overlooks his opponent's 17th move.

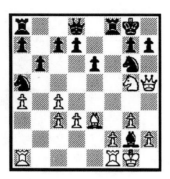

| **15...** | **h6** |
| **16.Qxg6** | **hxg5** |

And now 17.Kxg2! Qf6! was the last chance for equality.

| **17.Bxg5?** | **Be4!!** |
| **18.dxe4** | **Qe8** |

This was the point of Black's play. Although temporarily a pawn down, he can force a very favorable ending in which White's pawns are a mess.

19.Qxe8	**Raxe8**
20.Rad1	**d6**
21.c5	

This was White's best chance to resolve the Queenside at the least cost. Against quiet play (e.g. Kg2, h2-h4) Black will pick off the c4-pawn, play ...e6-e5 and begin to use the light squares (...Kf7-e6).

21...	**bxc5**
22.e5!?	**d5**
23.Rb1	**a6!**

Black had to stop Rb5 and 23...Rb8? 24.Be7! was not the way.

| **24.Be3** | **c4** |
| **25.f4** | |

This makes a bad Bishop worse but it was hard to suggest counterplay against the plan of ...Nb3/...c7-c5/...d5-d4.

| **25...** | **Nb3** |

26.Rf2	c5
27.Rc2	Rb8
28.Kg2	

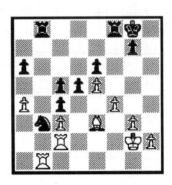

| 28... | Kf7! |

The King is headed toward the Queenside. White tries to create a passed Kingside pawn in response.

| 29.h4 | g6 |
| 30.Rcb2 | Rbc8 |

Not allowing any 31.Bxc5 tricks and guarding against Exchange sacrifices on b3.

31.Bf2	Ke7
32.Kf3	Kd7
33.Kg4	Rf5

This last move stops 34.h5 and paves the way for ...Kc6 followed by the advance of the d-pawn.

34.Kf3!?	Kc6
35.g4	Rf7
36.Rh1	Rcf8
37.Bg3	d4

Now 38.cxd4 Nxd4+ 39.Ke4 c3 provokes desperation.

| 38.Ke4 | dxc3 |
| 39.Rf2 | Rd7 |

40.h5	Rd3

White resigns

Black had 41...Nd2 + coming up.

18) Pestic-S.Bernstein, World Open 1978

1.Nf3	b6
2.g3	Bb7
3.Bg2	c5
4.d3	g6
5.0-0	Bg7

Black effectively takes aim at control of d4.

6.e4	Nc6
7.Nbd2	Nh6

There's nothing wrong with 7...e5 and ...Nge7 either, e.g. 8.Nc4 d6 9.a4 Nge7 10.c3 0-0 and ...f7-f5.

8.Nh4	0-0
9.f4	f5
10.e5	Qc7
11.Ndf3	

Wrong Knight. The one at h4 has done its duty and should be the one to occupy f3.

11...	Rad8
12.c3	Nf7

The Knight is well placed and with his next move Black prepares the maneuver ...Ne7-d5.

13.Re1	e6
14.d4?	

A typical error in more open 1...b6 positions, as we've seen. White should prepare this with 14.a3.

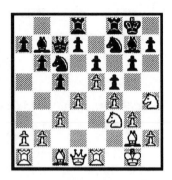

| 14... | cxd4 |
| 15.cxd4 | |

To late to back out with 15.Nxd4 Nxd4 16.Qxd4 because of the powerful 16...d6!.

15...	Nb4!
16.Re2	Ba6
17.Rd2	Rc8

Black has made excellent use of the weakened Queenside light squares. Now 18.Qa4 was probably best but...

18.a3	Nc2
19.Rb1	Ne3
20.Qb3	Qxc1 +!

A good solid investment for the Queen, considering how well this mock sacrifice exposes the many weaknesses in White's position.

| 21.Rxc1 | Rxc1 + |
| 22.Ne1 | |

Of course, 22.Kf2 Ng4 mate was unplayable.

22...	Rxe1 +
23.Kf2	Nxg2
24.Nxg2	Rf1 +
25.Ke3	Nh6!

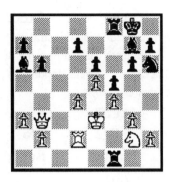

Black had several winning methods, including the domination of the c-file by his Rooks. He prefers a mating attack.

26.h3	g5!
27.Rd1	

Afterwards Black pointed out 27.fxg5 f4+! 28.Nxf4 Nf5+ 29.Ke4 d5+! and wins (30.Nxd5 Re1+ or 30.exd6 Nxd6+ 31.Ke3 Nc4+).

27...	g4!!
28.Rxf1	

Otherwise 28...Rf3+.

28...	Bxf1
29.Kf2	gxh3

The newly-created passed pawn becomes a monster.

30.Ne1	h2
31.Qf3	Bc4!
32.Qg2	Ng4+!

White resigns

Because of 33.Kf3 Bd5+. "If I live to be 100 I may never play such a game again," Sidney Bernstein said afterwards.

19) Hoffman-Soltis, New York 1978

1.Nc3	b6!
2.Nf3	Bb7

3.g3	**Bxf3!?**

The reasoning behind adopting this strategy here runs this way: White's first move has prevented him from easily advancing in the center with c2-c4 and d2-d4-d5. Therefore, Black messes up his opponent's pawns and builds his own phalanx on central light squares.

4.exf3	**e6**
5.Bg2	**Nf6**
6.0-0	**Be7**
7.b3	

If White is going to open the g2-a8 diagonal with f3-f4, he needs a better diagonal for the other Bishop.

7...	**0-0**
8.Bb2	**c6**
9.f4	**d5**

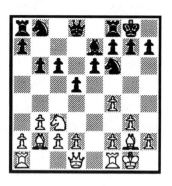

10.Re1	**Nbd7**
11.Qf3	

Since Black will attack on the Queenside, this attempt at generating Kingside action may be ill advised.

11...	**Bd6**
12.Ne2!	

The Knight, misplaced at c3, is headed for e5 via c1 and d3.

12...	**b5**

13.Nc1	Qa5
14.Qe2	Ba3!

Standard strategy: when your opponent has the two Bees, you want to exchange one of them.

15.Bxa3	Qxa3
16.Nd3	a5
17.h4	Rfe8!

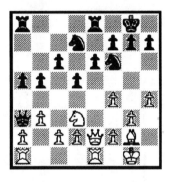

Black is preparing a Queenside attack with his c-pawn and therefore takes precautions on the Kingside first. With h7 looming as a target, he begins the overprotection of that square (...Nf8).

18.g4	g6
19.Bf3	c5
20.Ne5	c4
21.h5	Nxe5!
22.fxe5	Nd7

Despite appearances, White cannot exploit the holes at f6 and h6 and must try instead to attack along the h-file.

23.Kg2	Rec8
24.Rh1	cxb3
25.axb3	Qb2

Winning a pawn. No better was 25.cxb3 Rc2.

26.c3	Qxb3

27.Qe3	Qc4
28.hxg6	fxg6
29.Qg5	Nf8

This Knight defends the entire Kingside. Sacrifices on h7 or g6 are now White's only resource.

30.Rh6	Rc7
31.Re1	Rf7
32.Be2	Qc5
33.f4	b4
34.Bd3	Rg7!

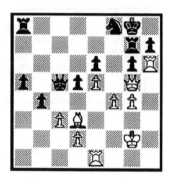

Rock-solid. Now the passed Queenside pawns cannot help but decide the game.

35.Reh1	bxc3
36.dxc3	Qxc3
37.R1h3	Qd2 +

White resigns

20) Kuligowski-Andruet, Dijon 1987

1.Nf3	b6
2.c4	Bb7
3.Nc3	e6

4.e4	**Bb4**
5.Bd3	**Ne7**

The pawn doubling plan of Bxc3 is dangerous to White because it leaves him with little in the way of line-opening middlegame plans. For example, 6.a3? Bxc3 7.dxc3 d6 8.0-0 Nd7 and Black will build an impregnable dark-square center.

In Gabriel-Kengis, 1990 Black's advantage was obvious after 9.Re1 0-0 10.Bg5 f6! 11.Bd2 Qe8 12.Nd4 Qf7 13.Qc2 Ne5 14.Bf1 c5! followed eventually by ...Qg6 and ...f6-f5.

6.0-0	**0-0**
7.Ne2?	

A better try besides 7.Re1, is 7.Bc2, clearing the way for the d-pawn to advance. Following 7...f5 8.exf5 Nxf5 White gets a fine position with 9.Ne4 Be7 10.d4 Nc6 11.d5 Nb4 12.Bb3 (Fedorowicz-Flear, Wijk aan Zee 1988).

Better may be 7...Bxc3 and then perhaps 8.bxc3 c5 and ...Nbc6-a5.

7...	**f5!**
8.Qc2	

The Knight at e2 interferes with White's other pieces (8.exf5 Bxf3).

8...	**Na6**
9.a3	**Nc5!**

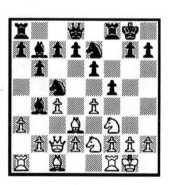

And now 10.axb4 Nxd3 11.Qxd3 fxe4 regains the piece favorably. White's seventh move has proven to be a disaster.

10.e5	**Bxf3**
11.gxf3	

White probably did not expect to win the trapped Bishop after 11...Nxd3 12.Qxd3 Bc5 13.b4.

11...	Nc6!
12.f4	

Not 12.axb4 Nxb4, regaining the d3-Bishop.

12...	Qh4!
13.Qb1	Qg4 +
14.Ng3	Nd4

Threatening, among other things, 15...Nf3 + , 15...Qf3 and 15...h5.

15.f3!?	Nxf3 +
16.Kg2	Nh4 +
17.Kh1	Qh3
18.Rf2	

Black's immediate threats are winding down but his Bishop is now saved with tempo – and a pawn profit.

18...	Nxd3
19.Qxd3	Bc5
20.Re2	Ng6

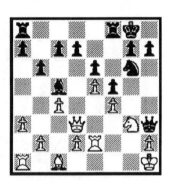

21.Qf3	Qg4

White resigns

21) Huebner-Miles, Bad Lauterberg 1976

1.c4	b6
2.e4	Bb7
3.Nc3	

An interesting choice by White who carefully avoids d2-d4.

3...	e6
4.Nf3	Bb4
5.Bd3	Ne7
6.0-0	0-0
7.Re1	f5
8.e5?	

Theory endorses 8.a3 Bxc3 9.dxc3, after which 9...fxe4 10.Bxe4 Bxe4 11.Rxe4 Nbc6 12.Nd4 is fairly level (12...Qe8 13.Qe2 a6 14.Nxc6 Nxc6 and a quick draw in Friedgood-Keene, Cape Town 1976).

8...	Ng6
9.Bf1	Bxf3!
10.Qxf3	Nc6

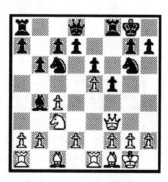

The threat of 11...Nd4, entombing White's pieces, as well as 11...Ngxe5, leads to early desperation.

11.d4!	Nxd4
12.Qd3	Nc6
13.f4	d6

Without this move, Black might be in trouble. Now, however, he reaches a favorable endgame.

14.exd6	**Qxd6**
15.Qxd6	**cxd6**

The endgame requires some exact technique but should be won (16.Rxe6? Nd4 17.Re1 Nc2 makes it easy).

16.Rd1	**Rad8**
17.Nb5	**Rd7**
18.a3	**Bc5 +**
19.Kh1	**d5**

This is one passed pawn that must be pushed.

20.b4	**Be7**
21.cxd5	**Bf6!**
22.Ra2	**cxd5**

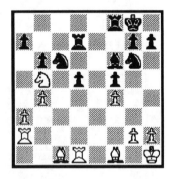

Black now consolidates his advantage by doubling Rooks, connecting Knights and moving his King to a dark (and thereby safer) square.

23.Rc2	**Nge7**
24.Be3	**Rfd8**
25.Kg1	**Kf8**
26.Nd4	**Nxd4**

A favorable trade of minor pieces frees Black's Rooks from the defense of Queenside targets.

27.Bxd4	**Bxd4 +**
28.Rxd4	**Rc8**

Now 29.Rxc8 + Nxc8 30.Bc4 Ne7 and ...Kf7-e6 wins.

29.Rcd2	**Rc1**
30.Kf2	**Rdc7**
31.Be2	**R1c2**

The exchange of one pair of Rooks makes the world safer for the Black King.

32.Bf3	**Rxd2 +**
33.Rxd2	**Rd7**
34.Re2	**Kf7**
35.g3	**g6**
36.Re5	

White defends well, requiring Black to find a new plan.

36...	**Rd6**
37.b5	**Kf6**
38.Ke3	

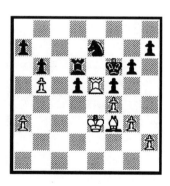

Perhaps 38.h4 was more accurate. Black now makes progress with:

38...	**d4 +!**
39.Kd3	**g5**

40.Kc4	**gxf4**
41.gxf4	**d3**

It's a runaway d-pawn. Now 42...Ng6 is coming up.

42.Re3	**Ng6**
43.Rxd3	**Rxd3**
44.Kxd3	**Nxf4 +**
45.Kd4	**Ke6**

White resigns

NOTES

NOTES

NOTES

NOTES